Copyright Compliance

FOR CHURCHES

A Quick
Reference Guide
for
Worship Leaders

WRITTEN BY
KIMRA MAJOR-MORRIS, ESQ.

LEGAL DISCLAIMER. Please note that the details included within this book are for informational purposes only. The publisher and author have made every effort to ensure the accuracy of the information contained within this book. However, they make no warranties as to the completeness of the contents herein, and hence hereby declaim any liability for errors, omissions, or contrary interpretation of the subject matter.

Published by: Pen Legacy Publishing

Library of Congress Cataloging – in- Publication Data has been applied for.

Hardback ISBN: 978-1-952903-20-5

E-Book ISBN: 978-1-952903-23-6

PRINTED IN THE UNITED STATES OF AMERICA.

Acknowledgements

I've been so privileged to have a personal and professional village who have enriched my experiences as a person and as an attorney. Robert Henley, "Thank You" for your encouragement to bring this book to life 11 years before the demand for e-worship services in the pandemic. I'm certain that I would not have completed it, or had the idea to conduct seminars on this topic without your advocacy within church technology departments.

To my parents, Betty and Lloyd Major, who laid the foundation for me to believe I can do anything I set my mind to - "Thank You" seems inadequate! Your love and endless support have been major keys to my success. To my two daughters, Sadé and Niara, who inspire me to be the best version of myself; you have helped me to show up consistently for all of us. To my big brother Anthony, "Thank You" for always going the extra mile to make sure I'm okay. To Clark, thank you for your unique support. It matters! My husband, Kwami – thank you for holding me up through the long and trying days; you magnify my strengths and remind me that the best things in life include love and peace of mind. I love you.

To my mentors, Attorneys Kendall Minter, Ava Doppelt, Dineen Wasylik, Ben Crump, Gregory Reed, and Steph Nagin, thank you for inspiring me, for pouring into me, sharing your wisdom, guiding me in my practice, and showing me to pay it forward. I appreciate you all.

To Yvette Harris and Leah Wilcox, Natalie Jackson, and Scharmaine Lawson, you have elevated my circle and my opportunities with your genuine enthusiasm and organic shares. Thank you!

To my clients over the last 13 years, I am grateful for you and look forward to adding value to your continued success.

Table of Contents

Introduction

As a copyright lawyer who's been advising clients in this field for over 45 years, I was thrilled to learn that Kimra was writing this book. There has long been a need for a good, accessible source of this kind of information, and that need has only increased as houses of worship have become more multimedia-oriented, especially when COVID forced many to hold their services online. Like so many other areas of the law, copyright law is frequently misunderstood and misapplied. Although there are certainly intentional offenders looking to take advantage of others' efforts, much of the activity that constitutes copyright infringement simply happens by mistake, out of ignorance of the law. Charitable, religious and educational institutions, unfortunately, are common offenders because they don't seek legal counsel and assume they are exempt from rules that apply to commercial ventures. I have had to remind people many times that there are individuals and businesses that are focused only on the church or school market, and they deserve protection too.

People want to do the right thing, and to know what the right thing is, in copyright as well as in the rest of life, and certainly this impulse pervades the faith-based community.

Kimra has written a highly useful, easy to digest book that every church, synagogue, mosque, or temple should own.

Ava K. Doppelt, Esq.

Chapter 1

WHO KNEW?

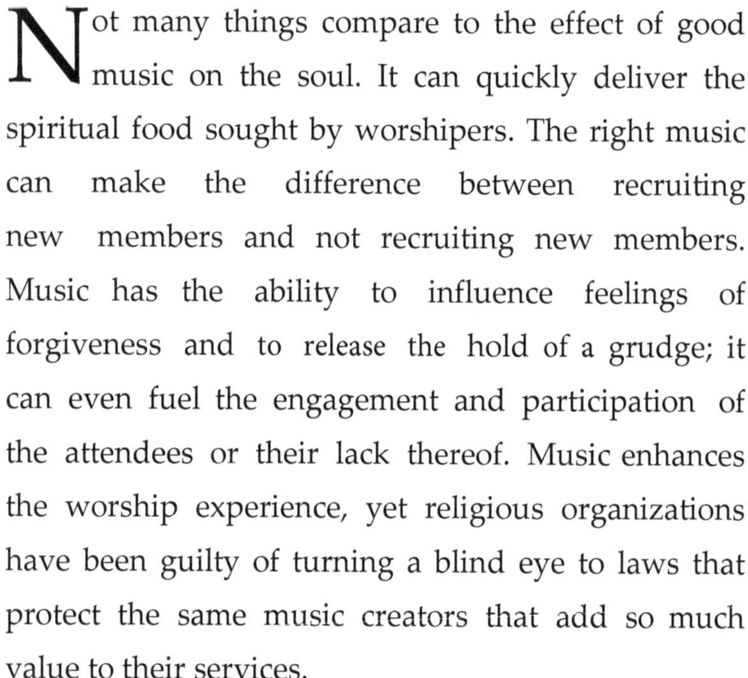

Not many things compare to the effect of good music on the soul. It can quickly deliver the spiritual food sought by worshipers. The right music can make the difference between recruiting new members and not recruiting new members. Music has the ability to influence feelings of forgiveness and to release the hold of a grudge; it can even fuel the engagement and participation of the attendees or their lack thereof. Music enhances the worship experience, yet religious organizations have been guilty of turning a blind eye to laws that protect the same music creators that add so much value to their services.

As a pastor's kid and choir member, it never occurred to me that recording or broadcasting the service could violate law. Prior to my law school attendance in 2004, I taught a college course about intellectual property's role in business and entertainment, but the *church copyright infringement light.*

didn't come on for me until early in 2008. Our church's music minister requested musical participants to provide a list of all musical selections to be performed during the service. The reason, he said, was for the church to make sure it complied with its broadcast license. There were only a few of us in attendance that night, and none of us posed a follow-up question for clarification. It probably went over most people's heads and I was too stunned to form a question, but I went home to research church copyright licenses.

How was it that I had just completed law school, earned an "A" in my copyright law class, taught a copyright law course, and didn't realize that various practices in religious organizations were subject to copyright infringement claims, until a church broadcast license was mentioned on a *single* occasion? How could I have missed the legal significance of the church's online music activities? We briefly touched on the religious service exemption in class, and I assumed that all religious activities were covered under it. If *I* missed it, I knew I wasn't the only one.

That was over a decade before COVID-19 made virtual worship services as common. With the drastic decrease of in-person services, musicians' and producers' earnings went down, and religious organizations are more vulnerable now than ever to potential copyright claims.

This book aims to inform organizational leaders of laws that protect authors of the music and literature that enhance worship experiences. If I surveyed twenty worship leaders and asked if they are guilty of weekly theft, the predictable response would be a resounding denial. However, if I surveyed twenty copyright holders and asked if religious organizations are among the main culprits of copyright infringement, an ugly reality would be revealed.

Why, then, are the lawsuits against religious organizations not flooding the courts – and why is news of the problem not dominating social media headlines? Would *you* file a lawsuit against *your* organization if you discovered it frequently performed songs or displayed, reproduced, edited, printed and distributed *your* work without asking or compensating you? Do you believe it's reasonable for gospel artists to sue religious organizations for infringement when those organizations are engaged in goodwill while using unauthorized creative works?

Each organization must consider these questions. Infringing on rights that are <u>exclusive</u> to copyright holders is stealing…using their intellectual property without permission.

Religious organizations should not wait to be 'called out' on copyright violations. We have a collective duty to educate ourselves to ensure against violating the law.

Chapter 2

COPYRIGHT LAW BASICS

Copyright laws are federal laws, contained in Title 17 of the United States Code. They protect the unique, *tangible* expression of ideas. Wondering how ideas become tangible? They become tangible when we memorialize them in writing, record them in digital format, photographs, or any concrete form. In other words, if you learn someone has launched a new project after you *imagined* it (but didn't produce it into a tangible form) before its release, you should not expect royalty checks from that project.

Once you've recorded your creation to a tangible form, you are recognized as the author of that work, with certain exclusive rights, for the rest of your life plus 70 years. Of course, whether you license or sell those rights or hold onto them for generational wealth building, is the author's decision to make. There are a few exceptions to this ownership right.

For example, if the work was the subject of a work for hire agreement, or if the work was performed within the scope of the author's employment, the copyright in the work will automatically belong to the employer rather than the creator.

A copyright owner is not required to register the copyright with the U.S. Copyright Office, but registration is required if you want to sue someone for infringement. Damages between $750 and $30,000 per infringement may be awarded by a court, and where willful infringement is found, fines up to $150,000 may be applied. While it's rare, courts also have ordered imprisonment for copyright violations.

Copyright laws provide incentive for individuals to create original works and be compensated for their creations. Would *you* be inspired to invest time, talent and financial resources in creative work so others may profit, without your own compensation or (even) credit? Not all authors want to monetize their work, but federal law requires most users of copyrighted works to at least obtain the owner's consent.

COPYRIGHT LAW BASICS

First, let's consider what works can be copyrighted. There are eight broad categories of copyrightable works:

- Literary works
- Musical works, including accompanying words
- Dramatic works, including accompanying music
- Pantomimes and choreographic works
- Pictorial, graphic and sculptural works
- Motion pictures and other audio-visual works
- Sound recordings
- Architectural works

Once an author saves his or her unique, creative expression in a tangible form, the author has six exclusive rights in that work. This means that the copyright owner automatically possesses rights in the work that, generally, no one else can use without permission. The copyright owner's exclusive rights are:

1. **To reproduce** the copyrighted work in copies or phonorecords
2. **To prepare derivative works** based upon the original copyrighted work

3. **To distribute copies or phonorecords** of the copyrighted work to the public by sale or other transfer of ownership, or by rental, lease, or lending
4. *In the case of literary, musical, dramatic, and choreographic works, pantomimes, and motion pictures and other audiovisual works,* **to perform** the copyrighted work publicly
5. In the case of literary, musical, dramatic and choreographic works, pantomimes, and pictorial, graphic or sculptural works, including the individual images of a motion picture or other audiovisual work, **to display** the copyrighted work publicly; and
6. *In the case of sound recordings,* **to perform** the copyrighted work publicly by means of digital audio transmission.

The most common abuse of copyrighted works in worship services is the direct violation of performance and display rights. Specific examples and suggested actions to avoid continued abusive practices are discussed in later chapters.

Chapter 3
PROPERTY OWNERS

We can never assume that the original author of the work is the current copyright owner. It would be the same to assume that an original homeowner still holds the deed to the same house long after it's built. To hold a copyright is to own an intellectual property asset. This chapter will explain how non-authors can become copyright holders of creative works.

As a reminder, with or without copyright registration, in most cases, the author is the original copyright owner. The six exclusive rights listed in Chapter 2 may be assigned, shared, terminated or expired.

If you are an employee and create original work as a part of your job, the copyright automatically belongs to the employer and you (the employee) have no rights in the work. On the other hand, if the work is created by an independent contractor, whether or not the contractor is paid, the contractor owns the copyright. If the commissioner of the work wants to own the copyright, the contractor must assign the copyright in writing or the contractor must sign a work-for-hire agreement. An example of this would be an organization contracting a music supervisor to write a theme song for the choir. The musician executes a work made for hire agreement and then delivers an original song for the choir.

One year later, the musician's relationship with the organization is terminated. If the musician would like to teach the same song to the choir at his new organization for an upcoming performance, he needs permission from the previous organization holding the copyright if the choir's performance of the song will be recorded or outside the place of worship. This is because (1) the musician has a signed work for hire agreement; (2) the previous organization owns all six exclusive rights to the song); and (3) the new organization must get written permission to perform the music outside a place of worship and to record the song.

Copyrighted works may be licensed for a period of time (often under publishing deals). The agreement between the parties might say that <u>all</u> six exclusive rights follow the new copyright holder, or it may only delegate a portion of the six rights and reserve the others rights for other licenses. Either way, this is an example of a non-author acquiring the rights in the work. All assignments are exclusive licenses that must be in writing and *should be* filed with the U.S. Copyright Office. Unfortunately, the copyright transfer recordation with the U.S. Copyright Office is a formality too often disregarded, and that makes it harder to find the actual copyright holder when searching.

It is not required for copyright owners to include the © symbol to prove ownership. Many unknowing infringers have fallen into the trap of "there is no proof of ownership, so it must be in the public domain," trap. A harmless chain email, image from Google, or devotional thought without an attribution to the author can easily be downloaded and forwarded, yet those who participate may not be considering the possible consequences. In a college course I taught, one of my students made this statement: "It doesn't feel like it's stealing because you just click on something and download it. It's not like going in a store and actually stealing something." What are your thoughts about this? Remember, creative content is born of people's unique gifts.

In a Florida case, a playwright thought a quiz she received in a chain email would be nice to add to the program for her show. Her quick online search for the author yielded no results only online copies of the same quiz. In addition, the answers to the quiz were so obvious that it was difficult for her to imagine that it would be problematic to include this entertaining quiz in the materials for patrons. Coincidentally, the author of the quiz attended one of the shows and noticed his work in the playbill – without attribution. He sued the playwright for copyright infringement, and she lost tens of thousands of dollars defending her case in court. Ultimately, the playwright prevailed because the court noted the author's implied consent for others to use the quiz and deemed the author's years of permissive behavior a bar to his recovery.

You should note that *intent* is not required for a party to be liable for copyright infringement. Innocent infringement is still infringement. Never assume that something is in the public domain (free to use without permission) because you've tried unsuccessfully to locate the author.

One other cause for the difficulty in identifying current copyright holder information is that authors forget to update their contact information with the Copyright Office.

Finally, as is common practice regarding other assets, copyright holders often make provisions for the transfer of ownership after their death through estate planning. A copyright owner's copyrights can be bequeathed just like any other assets, so that after death, the copyright will be managed and controlled by the beneficiary.

Chapter 4

FAIR USE OVERVIEW

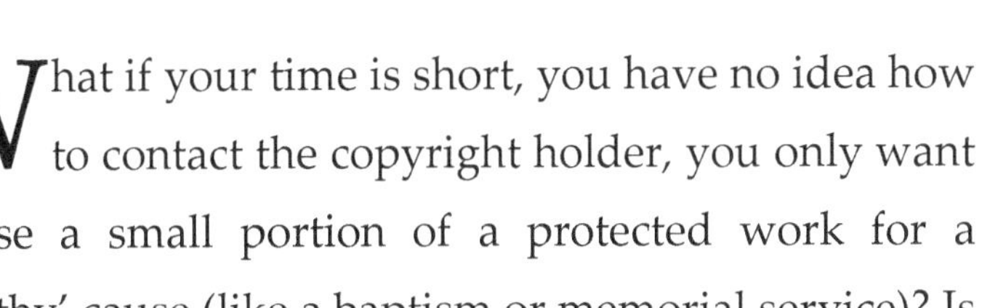

What if your time is short, you have no idea how to contact the copyright holder, you only want to use a small portion of a protected work for a 'worthy' cause (like a baptism or memorial service)? Is it against the law to borrow a segment to display or perform the material before an audience in need of it? Who decides when the use of the work *without* permission is acceptable?

The law does provide exceptions for the "fair use" of copyrighted works without permission. As you can probably guess, fair use isn't an automatic or simple defense. The fair use doctrine of the United States Copyright statute allows for the limited use of protected works in a few circumstances. As a general rule, the fair use doctrine does not protect the use of copyrighted works for commercial gain. The fair use doctrine mentions explicitly, as possible fair uses, using the work forncriticism, comment, news reporting, teaching (including multiple copies for classroom use), scholarship, or research. 17 U.S.C. § 107. The limitation on the use is key, because the copying of an entire work is one of the most identifiable disqualifying factors.

The categories specifically named do not suggest all the items to consider before assuming you can use protected works without permission. Copyright law lists four factors to be used in the balancing test that determine whether the use is fair. After all, this is no small thing. Remember, copyright holders, without the application of the fair use doctrine, have <u>unlimited</u> exclusive rights. The function of the fair use doctrine is to loosen restrictions while protecting copyright holders . The four factors to be considered for fair use are:

1. The purpose and character of the use, including whether such use is of a commercial nature or is for nonprofit educational purposes;
2. The nature of the copyrighted work;
3. The amount and substantiality of the portion used concerning the copyrighted work as a whole; and

4. The effect of the use upon the potential market for or value of the copyrighted work.

Published works more often qualify as fair use, because they "readily lend themselves to productive use by others" and are less protected. Sony Corp. of America v. Universal City Studios, Inc. 464 U.S. 417, 496 (1984). This can be compared to a scenario where a group creates an original song during their rehearsal one night. Subsequent use by a person outside the group for criticism, comment, news reporting, teaching, scholarship, or research would be less acceptable (because the work is original and unpublished).

Again, there's no solid formula for *knowing* that it's okay to use a protected work without permission. Sometimes people assume that merely crediting the author of the work will avoid infringement. If I stole your wallet and acknowledged that it was yours while spending the cash inside, would that address the harm? Similarly, acknowledgment of the owner of a work used without authorization, if permission was required, will not protect against infringement claims. At best, it could minimize the penalty.

Imaginative works receive a greater amount of protection than factually based works, as it pertains a to fair use analysis. Remember, it's creativity and originality that's promoted and protected by our intellectual property laws. For example, a purple and green dinosaur that sings is more imaginative than a bland dinosaur that simply walks in a forest.

For practical reasons, the law recognizes that blocking all uses of protected works would stifle the beneficial uses of protected works for society's good.

Chapter 5

ARE YOU EXEMPT?

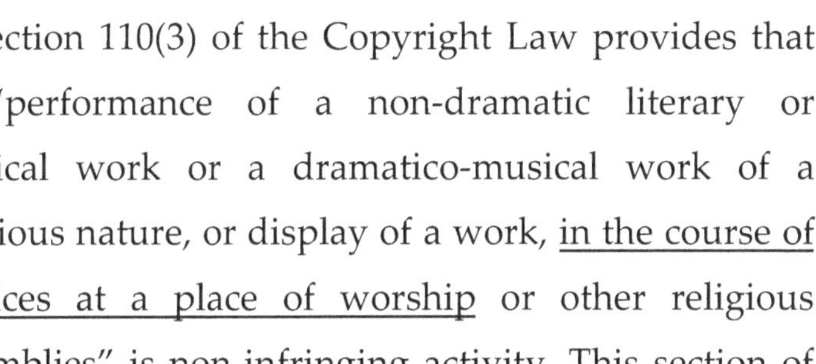

Section 110(3) of the Copyright Law provides that "performance of a non-dramatic literary or musical work or a dramatico-musical work of a religious nature, or display of a work, in the course of services at a place of worship or other religious assemblies" is non-infringing activity. This section of copyright law is known as the religious services exemption. Prior to the increase with sharing worship services through recording, broadcasting, distributing and selling unlicensed services and performances, the religious services exemption required much less attention.

Years ago, a typical worship service would have been attended live in a church, mosque, synagogue, or temple and not streamed online or broadcast on television. A simple piano or organ accompaniment would have enhanced the vocal performance of a hymn, and all musical performances were deemed non-infringing under the religious services exemption. Fast-forward to today's worship services – sent all over the world via the internet; lyrics projected on big screens, with people all over the world performing and viewing performances to soundtracks and remixes of protected works.

For that reason, church department leaders must be educated about likelihood of infringement in the context of recent technological advances, more music-driven services, and contractual arrangements between churches and outside companies.

The religious services exemption does not protect the unlicensed use of music performed during a worship service if the service is recorded, streamed, or broadcast. Remember, the copyright holder has the exclusive right to perform and distribute his work. However, when a service is broadcast, the broadcasting network is 'performing' a captured (recorded) work and distributing the work (outside the place of worship) when it transmits the service's broadcast. This is not common-sense, but unfortunately, ignorance of the law will not defend parishioners or the church (as a business entity) against liability.

Religious organizations are required to get the copyright owner's consent (a license) prior to the performance of any copyrighted work.

Chapter 6

LICENSE OVERVIEW

As changing technology continues to transform copyright law, churches (previously shielded by the religious service exemption, with simpler services) have begun to realize their vulnerability. With the addition of multimedia, the complexity of current church services has created fertile ground for copyright infringement claims. The riskiest issues arise with regard to the unauthorized use of music in worship services. Too often, religious organization leaders assume their use is protected under the religious services exemption.

Church copyright licenses were introduced in 1984. They are annual blanket licenses that churches may purchase to avoid having to secure individual permissions from copyright holders and publishers of protected works. For a flat fee determined primarily by the church's size, organizations can acquire licenses to perform copyrighted music at worship services for certain registered locations. They usually include the primary worship service venue and approved satellite campuses.

However, church copyright licenses leave numerous other issues in the gray area for church leaders who might reasonably believe all bases are covered with the performance license.

Here are some of the most common scenarios of infringement sometimes unresolved by a single church copyright license.

1. Performances

Scenario: The church just obtained a church copyright license and is now organizing a concert for the choir to sing ten of the songs included in the license. There are 50 choir members and the Minister of Music prints and hands out 50 copies of the lyrics for rehearsal.

However, the church has only acquired a duplication license to assist in congregational worship. In other words, the purchased license does *not* include a performance license for choirs. Rather, the duplication license only covers copying and viewing (not distributing physical copies of) words for congregational sing-alongs.

Note: *If the choir's concert occurs in a religious service, it does fall under the religious services exemption. If offsite or recorded, those uses are not necessarily covered. Read the license carefully to make sure the specific use is covered.*

2. Zoom (or other online platforms) Service

Scenario: Someone uploads a previously recorded worship service to the e-church Zoom meeting for the Zoom attendees' enjoyment. The previous recording was covered under the church's license.

Note: *While the church's performance license does allow for the taping and recording of live music to a device, internet broadcasts (or webcasts) require a separate broadcasting license, which is not covered by some licenses.*

Many organizations broadcast their services through third party companies but are required to first obtain a duplication license in addition to a broadcast license in order to webcast and archive performances from religious services and events.

3. Rehearsal CDs

Scenario: The music director advised that the choir needs to sing two extra songs in the next service. The director has two songs in mind, but choir members have to diligently listen and learn their parts before the next rehearsal. Between work schedules and family time, choir members always struggle to find time to listen to the suggested links on YouTube. With this in mind, the choir director purchased the two extra songs for 99 cents (each) from the iTunes store and burned a CD to distribute to each choir member for their convenience.

Note: *You might think this is acceptable because the songs were purchased. However, a single copy was purchased for private use. Had the choir director burned a CD for herself only, the user would have been protected. Imagine how much money songwriters and artists lose per adult choir, per youth choir, per children's choir, and per praise team!*

Each member must purchase downloads. Some choirs pay monthly dues to cover the cost of the musicians, robes, and travel expenses where applicable. It's a good idea to increase the cost of downloads or rehearsal CDs as a part of monthly dues.

4. **Accompaniment Tracks**

Scenario: The program for your service is already complete. The special music was planned over a week ago, but the musician has an emergency and needs to leave town the day before serve. The vocalist is notified that the pianist is not available to play the songs they've rehearsed. In response, the vocalist offers to bring an accompaniment track to perform the same song. It's agreed.

Note: *The problem is that the 'performance' of the accompaniment track is not covered under the church's copyright license. It is a license that must be negotiated separately. The accompaniment track was sold for private use, but the vocalist intends to use the track for a public performance. As a part of an unrecorded religious service, the public performance might be covered under the religious exemption. However, the capture and broadcast of the* *public performance falls outside the exemption. For the organization's protection, permission should be obtained for both uses. In this scenario, there is no time to obtain permission. Therefore, alternative (licensed) songs are recommended.*

5. **Handwritten (Published) Musical Arrangements**

   Scenario: It's time for the holiday program. The Minister of Music has expanded the choir to include singers and musicians from other churches for the performance of "Handel's Messiah." This is a complex piece of music, and it would be extremely helpful for the musicians (and vocalists who read music) to see the musical arrangement written out. It's time-consuming, but the musical director wants to be as thorough as possible to accommodate the visiting participants. He handwrites the score and gives a copy to each participant.

Note: *The copyright holder has the exclusive right to reproduce his work and distribute it. Both of these exclusive rights are violated in this scenario, because writing out sheet music is a reproduction. Ask, ask, ask!*

Additional note: Handel's Messiah is in the public domain, but every ***new arrangement*** *of music, even of music in the public domain, is protectable by copyright.*

6. Reproduced Audio Recordings

Scenario: One of the organization's members has a recording studio. The congregation's 'best' praise team has received so many compliments about their music, and they want to record a CD to give several members who have requested copies of their favorite songs.

The group schedules a session to record the requested, popular gospel songs with its own band. The lead singer sounds exactly like a known gospel artist on a well-known version of one of the songs. Once the recording session is complete, the CD is saved and duplicated for 50 people.

Note: *In the U.S., anyone can record a remake (also known as a cover song). However, a compulsory license notice should have been sent to the publisher at least 30 days prior to reproducing the song to put the owner on notice and to negotiate royalties and payment arrangements* *regarding downloads and profits (if any). It's our job to know the rules and follow them.*

7. **Use of Songs Not in the Organization's License**

Scenario: A visiting group performs the special music but performs a medley of unscripted songs as an introduction. None of the unscripted songs are covered under the organization's license.

Note: *The coverage provided by church copyright licenses has greatly expanded over the years. If your organization does not have a comprehensive license that is backed by the performance rights organizations (ASCAP, BMI, and SESAC),the organization is still potentially liable for unlicensed performances if they're recorded. Remember, the religious service exemption protects the use of copyrighted music in performances in a place of worship. This exemption does not apply to virtual uses of the music, because the language of the law is specific to places of worship. Places other than the main venue must be listed in the license. This scenario is not as common as it used to be, because many of the religious licensing entities have broadened their catalogs to include more music. However, in the instance where the catalog falls short, unless the group is performing its own original songs, the* *organization can either stop broadcasting during the group's performance or obtain advance notice of the songs the visiting group will sing to assure that the organization has a right to broadcast those songs. It is the only way to be sure all performances are authorized.*

8. Edited, Webcast, or Reproduced Video Clips

Scenario: During the main worship service, the pastor decides to show a clip he found online for demonstrative purposes. He only wants to show a snippet from the beginning and the middle and edits the needed portions for the sake of time. The edited clip is shown to the congregation during the service.

Note: *This is not protected under the religious services exemption and would be impermissible even if the video were not shown in the broadcasted service. Editing a video clip creates a derivative work, and only the author or one specifically permitted has the right to create derivative works.*

Additionally, the video's digital transmission (broadcasting) requires a separate license, which may be for videos shown in the service.

The video, once shown over the web, is considered a performance. It has also been reproduced and distributed to the public as a derivative work. Sometimes web users are permitted to download webcasts. At this point, you should refer to the copyright holder's six exclusive rights to see how many of those rights have been violated in this example.

Where copyright law exempts "performance of a non-dramatic musical work or a dramatico-musical work of a religious nature, or display of a work, in the course of services," <u>the showing of motion pictures or other audiovisual works is not exempt</u>.

What that means is, the organization can either purchase a video license or contact the video producer and distributor directly to obtain permission to use the video clip. The latter may be very time-consuming.

9. <u>Unauthorized Music Used with Video</u>

Scenario: Some of the children in the organization went on a camping trip to gain outdoor exposure, survival training and to build team-playing skills. Shortly after their return, the youth leaders created a video of the trip highlights and replaced the natural sound with popular music. The video was shown at a youth service.

Note: *Even where the organization licenses a piece of underlying music (used in the video), it is not permissible to synchronize the music with video under the same license. The author of the music must permit the synchronized music. The license you will need is called a sync license.*

Another example of unauthorized music joined to video is when 'praise dancers' perform to accompaniment tracks and the dance is synchronized to the music and recorded to another medium.

10. Protected Musical Works Used for a Commercial Purpose

Scenario: An artist in Powder Springs, Georgia wrote and produced a song that he shared with a friend. The friend then shared the song with his choir. The choir promoted and performed the original piece at a concert in which they also sang numerous other songs. An admission fee of $10.00 was charged to all who attended the event. The concert was recorded, and copies were sold immediately after the event.

Unbeknownst to the choir, the songwriter attended the concert and was furious when he saw that his music was being performed and sold without his consent. He filed a claim against the church and its representatives who organized the concert. The church paid the artist a settlement fee to avoid litigation.

Note: *Even if the concert had been free admission and the copies been given to attendees at no charge, the financial harm might still be an issue (because the market value of the copyrighted work may have been affected). The religious service's performance did not require permission under the exemption, but the recording, distribution, and sales require the copyright owner's consent.*

11. <u>Unauthorized Images Distributed or Sold</u>

Scenario: A religious service leader, in preparing a newsletter, downloaded a photograph from a Google search. He liked the letter's improved appearance and sent the draft to several committee members for their feedback. Not long afterward, he received notice from the agency that owned the image, notifying him that he had infringed on their copyright. The agency had embedded metadata in all of its images to track downloads and had traced the unauthorized use (the download and email distribution) of the image through the embedded code. The church member paid a settlement fee to the agency/publisher in the amount of $2,000 to avoid further legal consequences.

Note: *Online images are often mistaken as "free" images because they're so accessible. As the old saying goes, "Ignorance of the law is no excuse." Once downloaded, the violation has already occurred because the work is stored on the infringer's hard drive and maybe displayed or performed as often as the infringer chooses.*

12. Religious Organization's School Printing, Projecting or Recording Services

Scenario: One of the school teachers verified that the school choir would sing a song included in the organization's copyright license catalog. She printed the lyrics for the children to rehearse and planned to project the lyrics on the screen for audience participation at the graduation. The school hired a videographer to provide each parent a copy of the graduation video.

Note: *The church copyright license may not be transferable to the affiliated school and sharing may not be permissible. If not, the school is not authorized to distribute a song sheet handouts, project lyrics from the overhead slide projector or record the performance of protected music.*

13. Other Musical Performances

Whenever an establishment plays music for its patrons or members, it is considered a public performance of the music, and is unauthorized without a license. Examples of such 'performances' include the hold music played in virtual meetings (this also constitutes streaming, on the church's office phone, music played in the lobby before or after services, and music played at social gatherings or church- related events).

Check to see if your church copyright license covers such public performances. If not, performance licenses may primarily be obtained from performing rights organizations that represent songwriters or by contacting the author directly. ASCAP, for example, sells a "concert license" that covers hold music and lobby music. It also offers a license solely for hold music.

Chapter 7

FAQs

In conducting various workshops for church leaders and technology departments, I have addressed several concerns. Here are some of the most common questions and brief responses:

- ***A person at my church insists on recording the service each week, and we don't have a license. Is there something the church can or should do?***
  - The church should take steps to protect itself from vicarious liability for the infringing activities that occur online and on the premises. In other words, the church has a duty to oversee the people's actions under its copyright license, or it could be liable for contributing to infringement. For example, if the organization does not carry a license that allows for recording copyrighted works, it should forbid members and visitors from doing so.

- ***Is it okay for the choir to perform a concert and sell copies of the footage?***

As long as the church holds a license to perform and record the concert songs, the sale of DVDs or online access is the remaining issue. Companies have often negotiated flat rates with copyright owners to permit DVD and cassette sales for capped prices to a limited group of purchasers. For example, the maximum price permissible for a DVD sale might be $12.00, and the maximum price for a CD sale might be $4.00, under the same license.

- ***Some members are sick and shut-in. Is the church allowed to provide them with a copy of the service on DVD?***
    - The main purpose of a basic church copyright license is to encourage congregational participation. Therefore, if a church holds a license and some members are sick and cannot attend the service, the distribution of audio or video recordings to those individuals is not a violation of privileges under the license. This differs from situations where 'promotional' copies of services are distributed for

commercial gain. *(See Simpleville Music v. Jack Mizell in the Case Index).*

- ***I'd like to have my wedding at the church, with my friend singing to an accompaniment track. Is that okay? Do publishers make exceptions for these special occasions?***
    - Accompaniment tracks are not included in the licenses granted to religious organizations. While we hope this would be a permissible use by the publisher, it is a violation of copyright law not to have consent.
- ***I've been asked to show a PowerPoint presentation to the youth and want to include recent music to get their attention. What steps should I take to create a PowerPoint that's in compliance?***
    - Use music included in the templates, find royalty- free music, or get permission from the copyright owner. As an alternative, you might try websites that provide musical loops at minimal cost. The same applies to images used in the PowerPoint.

- ***This summer, we're planning a special service in the park. What restrictions are there regarding the music?***
    - Contact the license provider and purchase a mobile license, which should allow for printing songbooks, displaying protected content on the projector, and copyrighted songs' performance. Unfortunately, some mobile licenses do not allow for the recording or broadcasting of the service.
    - If it's a crusade or event other than the normal worship service, an event license purchased from the park/venue may be more accommodating and permissible for recording.
- ***The technology department wants to contract a graphic designer to revamp our website. How can we be sure the artwork is original and that we own the work upon completion?***
    - There are some safeguards the organization can take to ensure the work is original. The designer should sign warranties and representations that ensure he/she is the creator of the work. The designer should also agree to indemnify (pay for) anyone affiliated with the

organization in the event the organization is sued for using a copyrighted work without permission.

- Unless the designer was an employee, your organization's ownership of the work can only be acquired with an assignment of copyright from the designer to your organization. The law provides that an author may rescind (take back) the rights to his work after 30 years, and his termination rights cannot be waived by contract. This is currently an area of concern for many business owners who hold the rights to works assigned by the authors of corporate logos, theme songs, and other work associated with corporate brands.

➢ ***A service leader is always taking pictures of the congregation (or saving screenshots of the online service attendees). At least once, I've seen my picture in the newsletter. No one asked me. Can they do that?***

- To avoid this issue, the media department might require those who will be featured in publications to sign a photo release granting permission for such uses of your image.

- Also, note that an organization may claim an "implied copyright license" where regularly attending members are aware of weekly recordings and photographing during the service and still attend.
- Although the organization can claim copyright ownership in the photo, if the photos are used for commercial purposes without the permission of persons featured in the photos, the organization should be mindful of the state's publicity rights laws and privacy laws. Those laws vary by state.

➢ ***How can our organization protect its content? We have noticed that others repost and edit our content to attract viewers to their sites.***

- Use a (©) to put the public on notice.
- If you want to have the option to sue the infringer, register the work with the U.S. Copyright Office.

Chapter 8

CASE INDEX

Each featured case begins with a brief overview. Entire cases are included for the readers' benefit in focusing on copyright holders' claims and the Court's approach to deciding infringement cases.

The main purpose of this section is to raise awareness of infringement cases despite religious affiliation or intent by the infringer.

Featured cases are:

- Simpleville Music v. H. Jack Mizell (2006)
- Calhoun v. Lillenas Publishing (2002)
- Joel Songs v. Shelley Broadcasting Company (2007)
- Religious Technology Center v. Netcom Online Communication Services, Inc. (1995)
- Worldwide Church of God v. Philadelphia Church of God, Inc. (2000)
- Self-Realization Fellowship Church v. Ananda Church of Self Realization (2000)

CASE SUMMARY

(PAGES 43-52)

<u>**Simpleville Music v. H. Jack Mizell (2006)**</u> – ASCAP members sued the owner of radio stations for the unauthorized broadcasts of their copyrighted songs. This is a case where a radio station played "promotional CDs" on the air without paying royalties. The defendant thought that because his station played songs from promotional CDs, he didn't need to pay royalties. Stations that are given promotional CDs may distribute copies but may not broadcast them without paying royalties. The defendant also made the argument that the songs were "incidental" music and were used as bumpers and background music. Note: Even if music is incidental, it is not royalty-free. (Examples of incidental music include lobby music and hold music).

CASE LAW

451 F.Supp.2d 1293

SIMPLEVILLE MUSIC, et al., Plaintiffs, v.

H. Jack MIZELL, Defendant. Civil Action No. 1:04cv393-MHT. United States District Court, M.D. Alabama, Southern Division.

September 14, 2006.

Page 1294

Dylan Cook Black, James William Gewin, Bradley Scott Burleson, Bradley Arant Rose & White LLP, Birmingham, AL, Richard H. Reimer, American Society of Composers, Authors and Publishers, New York, NY, for Plaintiff.

Steve G. McGowan, Steve McGowan LLC, Dothan, AL, for Defendant.

OPINION

MYRON H. THOMPSON, District Judge.

The plaintiffs are members of the American Society of Composers, Authors and Publishers ("ASCAP"), to which they have granted a non- exclusive right to license public performances of their copyrighted musical compositions.[1] The plaintiffs

Page 1295

brought this lawsuit against defendant H. Jack Mizell, charging that he violated the Copyright. Act, 17 U.S.C. § 101-1332, by playing ASCAP's copyrighted musical compositions on the radio without authorization. This court has jurisdiction under 28 U.S.C. § 1338(a) (copyright) and § 1331 (federal question). Currently before the court is the plaintiffs' motion for summary judgment. The motion will be granted for the reasons that follow.

I. SUMMARY-JUDGMENT STANDARD

Summary judgment is appropriate "if the pleadings, depositions, answers to interrogatories, and admissions on file, together with the affidavits, if any, show that there is no genuine issue as to any material fact and that the moving party is entitled to a judgment as a matter of law." Fed.R.Civ.P. 56(c). Under Rule 56, the party seeking summary judgment must first inform the court of the basis for the motion, and the burden then shifts to the non-moving party to demonstrate why summary judgment would not be proper. *Celotex Corp. v. Catrett*, 477 U.S. 317, 323, 106 S.Ct. 2548, 91 L.Ed.2d 265 (1986); *see also Fitzpatrick v. City of Atlanta*, 2 F.3d 1112, 1115-17 (11th Cir.1993) (discussing burden-shifting under Rule 56).

The nonmoving party must affirmatively set forth specific facts showing a genuine issue for trial and may not rest upon the mere allegations or denials in the pleadings. Fed.R.Civ.P. 56(e).

The court's role at the summary-judgment stage is not to weigh the evidence or to determine the truth of the matter, but rather to determine whether a genuine issue exists for trial. *Anderson v. Liberty Lobby, Inc.*, 477 U.S. 242, 249, 106 S.Ct. 2505, 91 L.Ed.2d 202 (1986). In doing so, the court must view the evidence in the light most favorable to the non-moving party and draw all reasonable inferences in favor of that party. *Matsushita Elec. Indus. Co. v. Zenith Radio Corp.*, 475 U.S. 574, 587, 106 S.Ct. 1348, 89 L.Ed.2d 538 (1986).

II. FACTS

Mizell is the owner of Shelley Broadcasting, Inc. and Stage Door Development, Inc., and these two companies, in turn, operate radio stations WGEA and WRJFM, respectively. On September 20 and 21, 2003, WGEA broadcasted seven of the plaintiffs' ASCAP copyrighted compositions, and, on September 21 and 22, WRJM- FM broadcasted an additional eight.

Neither station had ASCAP's permission to perform these compositions.

The 15 broadcasted songs are "I Can Only Imagine," "Any Day Now," "Stranger In My House," "Walking In Memphis," "Lovin' All Night," "Maybe God Is Tryin' To Tell You Somethin'," "His Hand In Mine," "More Than Wonderful," "Above All," "Love Is Alive," "L.A. Woman," "Hip To Be Square," "Highway To Hell," "Smokin'," and "Luck Be A Lady Tonight."

III. DISCUSSION

To establish a prima-facie copyright infringement case for a musical composition, a plaintiff may prove (1) ownership of a valid copyright and (2) "public performance" of the copyrighted work without authorization. 17

U.S.C. § 106(4) (subject to other provisions in the Copyright Act that provide that certain uses of copyrighted materials are not infringements despite § 106, "the owner of copyright . . . has the exclusive rights . . . in the case of . . . musical . . . works . . . to

Page 1296

perform the copyrighted work publicly"); *cf.* *Feist Publications, Inc.*

v. Rural Telephone Service Co., Inc. 499 U.S. 340, 361, 111 S.Ct. 1282, 113 L.Ed.2d 358 (1991) ("To establish infringement, two elements must be proven: (1) ownership of a valid copyright, and

(2) copying of constituent elements of the work that are original."); *A & M Records v. Napster, Inc.*, 239 F.3d 1004, 1013 (9th Cir.2001) ("Plaintiffs must satisfy two requirements to present a prima facie case of direct infringement: (1) they must show ownership of the allegedly infringed material and (2) they must demonstrate that the alleged infringers violate at least one exclusive right granted to copyright holders under 17 U.S.C. § 106.").

The plaintiffs have satisfied the first element by submitting copies of the copyright registration certificates. *See* 17 U.S.C. § 410(c) ("In any judicial proceedings the certificate of a registration made before or within five years after first publication of the work shall constitute prima facie evidence of the validity of the copyright and of the facts stated in the certificate.").

With regard to the second element, the plaintiffs have presented the affidavits of Jerry Glaze, who recorded the broadcasts of radio stations WGEA and WRJM-FM on the days in dispute, and Alex Kuzyszyn, who listened to the tapes and identified that the 15 compositions constituting the basis of this suit were found on the tape recordings. The evidence supplied by Mizell, either admits that these compositions were broadcast on radio stations WGEA and WRJM-FM or concedes that they may have been played. And the law is settled that a radio broadcast constitutes a "performance" within the meaning and coverage of copyright law.

Twentieth Century Music Corp. v. Aiken, 422 U.S. 151, 161, 95 S.Ct.

2040, 45 L.Ed.2d 84 (1975) ("Broadcasters perform."); 2 Melville

B. Nimmer & David Nimmer, *Nimmer on Copyright* § 8.14[B][1] (2006) ("the act of broadcasting a work is itself a performance of that work"); *see also* 17

U.S.C. § 101 ("To `perform' a work means to recite ... it, either directly or by means of any device or process . ."). Mizell also admits that he did not have permission from the plaintiffs or ASCAP to broadcast the 15 songs.

However, Mizell asserts an array of defenses to the copyright claims.

He argues that there was no infringement because (1) the compositions were played from promotional CDs; (2) the compositions were played as incidental, background, or bumper music;[2] (3) the composition performers were not ASCAP members;

(4) the compositions fall within the religious exemption to copyright laws; (5) he did not intend to violate copyright laws; and (6) he did not personally control the content of the broadcasts. Mizell also requests a jury trial so that it may determine the appropriate amount of statutory damages. The court will discuss the validity of each defense.

1. Promotional CDs

Mizell contends that he could play the songs without permission because they came off promotional CDs. According to him, his stations have had a policy of playing only promotional, royalty-free music since 1991, and the ASCAP songs he played came from free CDs the radio stations received, royalty-free, from either Compact Disc Xpress (CDX) or Crossroads.[3] Promotional CDs are CDs that

Page 1297

are distributed for free and for which the writer and publisher will not collect royalties. 6 Melville B. Nimmer & David Nimmer, *Nimmer on Copyright* § 30.02 (2006).

However, the fact that a copyright holder grants recording companies the right to make and distribute promotional copies of their songs does not mean that it waives its right to collect fees when a radio station wishes to broadcast publicly from the promotional copy. *Chappell & Co. v.*

Middletown Farmers Market & Auction Co., 334 F.2d 303, 305 (3rd Cir.1964) ("The surrender of one monopoly—the right to make mechanical reproductions—does not carry with it the right to publicly perform the copyrighted musical composition.").

Moreover, while Mizell provides multiple examples of music subscription service's that pay the licensing fees for the subscriber,[4] none of these examples includes CDX or Crossroads, the two publishers of the CDs Mizell contends are promotional. In fact, the copies of the CD sleeves that accompanied the CDX CDs include the following cautionary language: "NOT FOR SALE: for promotional use only. Warning all rights reserved. Unauthorized duplication is a violation of applicable law."[5]

It is apparent that Mizell is using the term "promotional" out of context. The language on the CD sleeve defines the terms of its free, but restricted, transfer. The CD itself is promotional, its licensing for public performance is not. A radio station that receives a CD labeled "for promotional use only," which means that the station did not have to pay for the CD, must still obtain permission before broadcasting its contents. *See Chappell,*https://apps.fastcase.com

/Research/Pages/Document.aspx?LTID=
IqNdtpNOgzKX3GKWD
KPWU5YEu9750kGoaAbxOrdIp4DZyocomkZot
lFCSk9KUqE13
SQunG%2bQr9tT24enQSgvvzEGzwe4HmguVVjI2pp
YH EzNrCp
FyJCx94sXwBfYdspG&ECF=334+F.2d+at+305 334 F.2d at 305.

Mizell's promotional-CD defense is meritless.

2. Incidental or Background Use

Mizell used several ASCAP songs as background or bumper music. He asserts that, because ASCAP does not pay royalties to its members for background, bumper, or other incidental uses, he may use those songs as such without paying any licensing fees.

Background music is not exempt from being subject to licensing fees. *See Schumann v. Albuquerque Corp.*, 664 F.Supp. 473, 477 (D.N.M.1987) (Bratton, J.) ("The fact that the song might have been used as background to a community calendar does not render its performance fair use under § 107."). Additionally, courts do allow incidental use fees. *See United States v. American Socy. of Composers*, 981 F.Supp. 199 (S.D.N.Y.1997) (Conner, J.) (ASCAP's incidental use fee of 0.06% is reasonable). Mizell's background-use defense is meritless.

3. Non-ASCAP Performers

Mizell argues that the plaintiffs cannot claim copyright infringement when the performers of the offending compositions are not ASCAP members.

The copyright owner has an interest in the composition itself, regardless of the performer. 17 U.S.C. § 501(b). "The legal or beneficial *owner* of an exclusive right under a copyright is entitled, subject

Page 1298

to the requirements of [17 U.S.C. §]411, to institute an action for any infringement of that particular right committed while he or she is the owner of it." *Id.* (emphasis added). Mizell's non-ASCAP- performer defense is meritless.

4. Religious Exemption

Mizell argues that the `religious exemption' allowed him to broadcast some of the copyrighted compositions because they were performed during church services. 17 U.S.C. § 110(3) creates an exemption to copyright-law requirements for the "performance of a nondramatic literary or musical work or of a dramatico-musical work of a religious nature, or display of a work, in the course of services at a place of worship or other religious assembly."

The critical language here is "at a place of worship or other religious assembly"; the exception says nothing about broadcasts in general and, more specifically, broadcasts from a place of worship. True, it could be argued the exemption should apply where, although the songs are being broadcast, there is an audience at the place of worship; in short, the exemption, it could be argued, should apply because the conditions to the exemption have been satisfied. Thus, it could be argued, the exemption should apply to all simultaneous performances as long as one of the performances falls within the exemption.

However, the law is clear that radio broadcasting is itself a separate public performance which can constitute an infringement. *Twentieth Century Music Corp. v. Aiken,* 422 U.S. 151, 161, 95 S.Ct. 2040, 45 L.Ed.2d 84 (1975) ("Broadcasters perform."); 2 Melville B. Nimmer & David Nimmer, *Nimmer on Copyright* § 8.14[B][1] (2006) ("the act of broadcasting a work is itself a performance of that work"); *see also* 17

U.S.C. § 101 ("To `perform' a work means to recite . . . it, either directly or by means of any device or process"). Thus, the mere fact that a radio

broadcast of a song is simultaneous with the playing of the song at a place of worship does not mean that broadcast falls within the religious exemption; playing to the audience at the place of worship and playing to a broadcast audience are separate public performances. *See* H.R.Rep. No. 94-1476, at 55 (1976), *reprinted in* 1976 U.S.C.C.A.N. 5659, 5668 ("[A] singer is performing when he or she sings a song; a broadcasting network is performing when it transmits his or her performance; a local broadcaster is performing when it transmits the network broadcast; a cable television system is performing when it retransmits the broadcast to its subscribers."); *see also, Schumann v. Albuquerque Corp.,* 664 F.Supp.

473, 475 (D.N.M.1987) (Bratton, J.) (radio broadcast is a separate performance from live performance).

This understanding of the religious exemption is supported by its legislative history, which provides that the exemption does "not extend to religious broadcasts or other transmissions to the public at large, even where the transmissions were sent from the place of worship." H. Rep. No. 94-1476, at 84, *reprinted in* 1976 U.S.C.C.A.N. at 5698-99.

Accordingly, the court concludes that the religious exemption does not allow Mizell to broadcast copyrighted songs, performed during church services, without authorization, for such broadcasts are not "at a place of worship". *Id.* Mizell's religious-exemption defense is meritless.

5. Lack of Intent

Mizell protests that he did not intend to play copyrighted material and took measures to protect against such infringements. However, "intention to infringe is not essential under the [Copyright] Act." *Buck v. Jewell-LaSalle Realty* Co., 283 U.S. 191, 198, 51 S.Ct. 410, 75 L.Ed. 971

Page 1299

(1931). *See* U.S. Songs, Inc. v. Downside Lenox, Inc., 771 F.Supp. 1220, 1228 (N.D.Ga.1991) (Hall, J.) ("[T]he law is clear that lack of intent to infringe does not shield the infringer from liability."); 4 Melville B. Nimmer & David Nimmer, *Nimmer on Copyright* § 13.08 (2006) ("In actions for statutory copyright infringement, the innocent intent of the defendant will not constitute a defense to a finding of liability.").

Admittedly, five of the songs in this case were broadcast during syndicated radio shows, while one song was broadcast as part of a national television commercial. Nevertheless, "a broadcaster who is aware of his obligations under copyright law remains responsible for ensuring that copyrighted music is not aired without permission." *Jobete Music Co., Inc. v. Johnson Communications,* Inc., 285 F.Supp.2d 1077, 1089 (S.D.Ohio 2003) (Rice, C.J.) (where defendant was liable for copyright infringement for airing an NBC commercial that played "This Will **Be** (An Everlasting Love)" in the background without permission). Although Mizell did not produce the commercial or the radio shows himself, he was still responsible for ensuring that all of the licensing fees were paid. Consequently, Mizell's no-intent defense is meritless.

6. Personal Participation in Infringement

Mizell denies liability on the ground that he did not personally participate in the infringement. However, as the president, owner, and sole stockholder of the companies that own WGEA and WRJM- FM, he is liable for any infringement occurring at the stations. A person "including a corporate officer, who has the ability to supervise infringing activity and has a financial interest in that activity, or who personally participates in that activity is personally liable for the infringement." *Southern Bell Tel. & Tel. Co. v. Associated Tel. Directory Publishers,* 756 F.2d 801, 811 (11th Cir.1985) (citation omitted); *see also* *Chi-Boy Music v. Towne Tavern, Inc.,* 779 F.Supp. 527, 530 (N.D.Ala.1991) (Hancock, J.). Similarly, "under the Copyright Act, an individual who is the dominant influence in a corporation, and through his position can control the acts of that corporation, may be held jointly and severally liable with the corporate entity for copyright infringements, even in the absence of the individual's actual knowledge of the infringements."

Quartet Music v. Kissimmee Broadcasting, Inc., 795 F.Supp. 1100, 1103 (M.D.Fl.1992) (Kellam, J.).

The record is clear that Mizell fits the bill of being the supervising, dominant figure at the two radio stations.

Mizell's no-personal-participation defense is meritless.

7. Judge or Jury Trial

Mizell demands a jury on damages. 17 U.S.C. § 504(c) explains that "an infringer of copyright is liable for either—(1) the copyright owner's actual damages and any additional profits of the infringer, as provided by subsection (b); or (2) statutory damages, as provided by subsection (c).1" Subsection (c) further details that a "copyright owner may elect, at any time before final judgment is rendered, to recover, instead of actual damages and profits, an award of statutory damages . . . with respect to any one work . . . of not less than $ 750 or more than $ 30,000 as the court considers just."

Although the statute itself does not require a jury trial, the Supreme Court has held that "the Seventh Amendment provides a right to a jury trial on all issues pertinent to an award of statutory damages under § 504(c) of the Copyright Act, including the amount itself." *Feltner v. Columbia Pictures Television, Inc.,* 523 U.S. 340, 355, 118 S.Ct. 1279, 140 L.Ed.2d438 (1998).

Page 1300

The plaintiffs argue that a jury trial is unnecessary because they will accept the minimum statutory award of $ 750 per violation. "*Feltner* establish[ed] . . . that cases under § 504(a) are normal civil actions subject to the normal allocation of functions between judge and jury." *BMG Music v. Gonzalez,* 430 F.3d 888, 892 (7th Cir.2005), *cert. denied,* U.S._, 126 S.Ct. 2032, 164 L.Ed.2d 782 (2006).

"When there is a material dispute of fact to be resolved or discretion to be exercised in selecting a financial award, then either side is entitled to a jury; if there is no material dispute and a rule of law eliminates discretion in selecting the remedy, then summary judgment is permissible." *Id.* at 892-893.

Here, because the plaintiffs are seeking the statutory minimum and because the plaintiffs are asserting only one violation per song and because the record establishes as a matter of law that the violations occurred, the law has eliminated any discretion as to damages, and summary judgment is appropriate. *See id.* (holding that, because there were no disputed facts as to the statutory minimum award, summary judgment was proper as to damages); *Lava Records, LLC v. Ates,* No. Civ.A.05-1314, 2006 WL 1914166, at *3 (W.D.La. July 11, 2006) (James, J.) (finding that because the plaintiffs sought only the minimum statutory amount and courts have routinely held that an award of $ 750.00 per work is appropriately awarded by summary judgment, there was no need for jury trial on the issue of damages); *Capitol Records v. Lyons,* No. CivA.3:03-C2018-L, 2004 WL 1732324, at *3 (N.D.Tex. Aug.2, 2004) (Ramirez, Mag. J.) (finding that no hearing was necessary prior to an award of the minimum $ 750.00 per work where defendant defaulted and his acts of infringement were deemed admitted).

In short, because there is nothing for a jury to decide here as to damages, a jury is unnecessary.

8. Injunctive Relief

The plaintiffs request that the court permanently enjoin Mizell from publicly performing the 15 songs. While the court may grant a permanent injunction "on such terms as it may deem reasonable to prevent or restrain infringement of a copyright," 17 U.S.C. § 502(a), that grant is not unlimited; the court may, as a general matter, do so only when there is a substantial likelihood of further infringement of a plaintiff's copyrights. 4 Melville B. Nimmer & David Nimmer, *Nimmer on Copyright* § 14-06[B] (2006); *see also* *U.S. Songs, Inc. v. Downside Lenox, Inc.,* 771 F.Supp. 1220, 1229 (N.D.Ga.1991) (Hall, J.).

The record, on the plaintiffs' summary-judgment motion, is unclear whether Mizell's failure to honor the plaintiffs' copyrights was in good or bad faith. The court therefore believes that the prudent course to follow is to have an evidentiary hearing specifically addressing whether injunctive relief is needed and, if so, what form that relief should take. Of course, this assumes that the plaintiffs still want such relief in the wake of the final judgment entered today.

Therefore, the plaintiffs will have seven days from the date of this opinion to inform the court in writing if they want such relief, and, if they do, the court will set the matter down for an evidentiary hearing. If the plaintiffs fail to make this request within the time allowed, the court will assume that they have abandoned such relief.

IV. CONCLUSION

Because the plaintiffs have proven each of the elements of copyright infringement as to each of the 15 songs, and because Mizell has failed to offer valid defenses, an

Page 1301

appropriate summary judgment in favor of the plaintiffs will be entered. The assessment will be the minimum statutory fee of $ 750 for each of the 15 infringements, for a total of $ 11,250 (15 × $ 750 = $ 11,250).

JUDGMENT

In accordance with the memorandum opinion entered this date, it is the ORDER, JUDGMENT, and DECREE of the court that:

CASE INDEX

1. The motion for summary judgment filed by plaintiffs Simpleville Music, New Hidden Valley Music Co., BMG Songs, Inc.; Famous Music Corporation, Sony/ATV Tunes LLC, WB Music Corp., Lanny Wolfe Music Company, Integrity Music, Inc. d/b/a Integrity's Hosanna Music, Lensongs Publishing, Universal-MCA Music Publishing, a Division of Universal Studios, Inc., Doors Music Company, Hulex Music/WB Music Corp., J. Albert & Son (USA) Inc., and Pure Songs and Frank Music Corp. (Doc. No. 55) is granted.
2. Judgment is entered in favor of plaintiffs Simpleville Music, New Hidden Valley Music Co., BMG Songs, Inc.; Famous Music Corporation, Sony/ATV Tunes LLC, WB Music Corp., Lanny Wolfe Music Company, Integrity Music, Inc. d/b/a Integrity's Hosanna Music, Lensongs Publishing, Universal- MCA Music Publishing, a Division of Universal Studios, Inc., Doors Music Company, Hulex Music/WB Music Corp., J. Albert & Son (USA) Inc., and Pure Songs and Frank Music Corp. and against defendant H. Jack Mizell.
3. Plaintiffs Simpleville Music, New Hidden Valley Music Co., BMG Songs, Inc.; Famous Music

Corporation, Sony/ ATV Tunes LLC, WB Music Corp., Lanny Wolfe Music Company, Integrity Music, Inc. d/b/a Integrity's Hosanna Music, Lensongs Publishing, Universal-MCA Music Publishing, a Division of Universal Studios, Inc., Doors Music Company, Hulex Music/WB Music Corp., J. Albert & Son (USA) Inc., and Pure Songs and Frank Music Corp. shall have and recover from defendant Mizell the sum of $ 11,250.00.

4. Any request for injunctive relief must be filed by no later than September 21, 2006.
5. Any request for attorneys' fees and expenses must be filed by no later than September 28, 2006.

It is further ORDERED that costs are taxed against defendant Mizell, for which execution may issue.

The clerk of the court is DIRECTED to enter this document on the civil docket as a final judgment pursuant to Rule 58 of the Federal Rules of Civil Procedure.

CASE SUMMARY

(PAGES 54-73)

Calhoun v. Lillenas Publishing (2002) – Calhoun, a part-time organist who once worked at King's Temple Church, sued an associate pastor at King's Temple for copyright infringement. The associate pastor at King's Temple Church wrote the song "Emmanuel", which was licensed to dozens of companies and sounded similar to Calhoun's work. In this case, no copyright infringement was found, after the appeals court held that the associate pastor created the song independently, without copying from Calhoun's song (although it was very similar).

CASE LAW

RONALD G. CALHOUN, Plaintiff-Appellant, v.

LILLENAS PUBLISHING, Defendant-Third-Party Plaintiff, NAZARENE PUBLISHING BEACON HILL MUSIC, et al.,

Defendants-Appellees,

LIFEWAY CHRISTIAN RESOURCES OF THE SOUTHERN

BAPTIST CONVENTION, f.k.a. the Sunday School Board of the Southern Baptist Convention, d.b.a. Lifeway Christian Stores, CONVENTION PRESS, et al.,

Defendants-Appellees,

C.A. MUSIC, INC., Third-Party-Defendant-Appellee.

RONALD G. CALHOUN, Plaintiff-Appellant, v.

THE SOUTHERN BAPTIST CONVENTION LIFEWAY

CHRISTIAN RESOURCES, d.b.a Lifeway Christian Stores, THE SUNDAY SCHOOL BOARD OF THE SOUTHERN BAPTIST CONVENTION, et al.,

Defendants-Cross Claimants-Appellees,

THE UNITED METHODIST PUBLISHING HOUSE, COKESBURY PUBLISHING, et al., Defendants-Appellees. Nos. 01-11413, 01-11415

UNITED STATES COURT OF APPEALS FOR THE ELEVENTH CIRCUIT July 23, 2002

Appeals from the United States District Court for the Southern District of Georgia

Before BIRCH, CARNES and COX, Circuit Judges. PER CURIAM:

This consolidated appeal arises out of a putative copyright infringement action. In his pro se action, the gravamen of which focuses upon ownership of a musical work, Ronald Calhoun appeals the district court's grant of summary judgment in favor of Lillenas Publishing Company, Nazarene Publishing House, Beacon Hill Music, Crystal Sea Recordings, Faith Music, Pilot Point Music, Psalmsinger Music, Zondervan Publishing House, John Mathias, Hardy Weathers, and Ken Bible(FN1), docketed as our case No. 01- 11413, and The Southern Baptist Convention, Lifeway Christian Resources, The Sunday School

Board of the Southern Baptist Convention Press, Broadman & Holman, Baptist Book Stores, The United Methodist Publishing House, Cokesbury Stores, Christian Copyright License International, World Music, Nelson/Word Ministry Services, Maranatha Music, Integrity Music, Integrity Church Services, Music Services, Christian Artist Music (C.A. Music), Cam Floria, Jeffery Buchan, and Bob McGee (hereinafter collectively referred to as "McGee/Assigns"), docketed as our case No. 01-11415. The district court found that Calhoun had no claim for copyright infringement because there was insufficient evidence to show that (1) McGee had access to Calhoun's song "Before His Eyes," and (2) McGee's chorus "Emmanuel" was strikingly similar to "Before His Eyes." We AFFIRM the district court's judgment, albeit upon another basis.(FN2) We conclude that the evidence compels the conclusion that Calhoun's copyright claims should be barred by McGee/Assigns' claim of independent creation.(FN3)

I. BACKGROUND

Calhoun wrote the song "Before His Eyes" in 1969.(FN4) He recorded an album containing "Before His Eyes" on the Charisma record label in 1970, and it was subsequently released to the public for sale and distribution.

Calhoun has no records of any royalties from the album.

In March of 1971, Calhoun received a writer's clearance of his composition stamped and registered with the licensing performance agency Broadcast Music Incorporated ("BMI"). BMI cleared and announced the work in their forthcoming bulletins to stations. Calhoun promoted and performed this musical work by means of concerts, and performances in churches, and on television and radio. However, the total amount of royalties Calhoun has received to date is $11.

In 1976, Robert McGee, then an associate pastor at The King's Temple Church(FN5) in Seattle, Washington, wrote the chorus "Emmanuel." The chorus first appeared in a collection of 11 choruses entitled Choruses From The King's Temple, 1976 Book I and was used by the church in their worship services. In 1983, C.A. Music, Inc. acquired the copyright in "Emmanuel" and licensed the song to dozens of companies. To ensure proper title to the copyright in "Emmanuel," C.A. Music acquired several affidavits from eye witnesses who testified that they watched McGee independently create the song. R3-69-3. Since then, "Emanuel" has appeared in a number of Christian denomination hymnals, and has been translated into dozens of foreign languages. For much of the 1980s and 1990s, it was ranked in the top 20 requested songs rated by Christian Copyright Licensing, Inc., a copyright clearinghouse company that monitors and reports licensing transactions for Christian music.

From 1989 until 1998, Calhoun was a part-time organist at a United Methodist Church. As an organist, he played for choir rehearsals three times a week and played from hymnals which included "Emmanuel." He admits to using these hymnals, but Calhoun contends that he did not discover "Emmanuel" until 1997.

On 19 July 1999, Calhoun filed a pro se complaint for copyright infringement in the Southern District of

Georgia against various publishing houses and record labels. Calhoun alleged that the chorus "Emmanuel" was based on the chorus section of "Before His Eyes," and that McGee/Assigns published, marketed, promoted, and distributed the alleged infringing work without Calhoun's permission. Calhoun filed a second complaint on 30 March 2000 against various publishing houses, churches and Christian book stores. The district court consolidated both actions, noting that the claims were identical.

McGee/Assigns moved for summary judgment arguing that McGee independently created and had no reasonable access to "Before His Eyes" when he created "Emmanuel." They further argued that "Emmanuel" was not substantially similar to "Before His Eyes" because the lyrics, chord progressions, and keys of the two compositions were different.

Additionally, McGee/Assigns asserted that McGee's action was barred by the three-year statute of limitations and the equitable doctrine of laches, due to his long delay in filing suit.

Calhoun responded by asserting that McGee had access to "Before His Eyes" because it was promoted at concerts, churches, television, and radio stations. Further, he contended that the two works were strikingly similar and that the delay and laches arguments were without merit because he first discovered the alleged infringement in 1997, within the three-year statute of limitations for filing this action.

The district court granted McGee/Assigns' motion for summary judgment finding that there was insufficient evidence to show both access and striking similarity. The district court did not alternatively consider McGee/Assigns' statute of limitations, delay, and laches arguments.

Calhoun filed a timely appeal of the judgment.

II. DISCUSSION

We review a district court's grant of summary judgment de novo, apply the same standard as the district court, and review all facts and reasonable inferences in light most favorable to the nonmoving party. <u>Allison v.</u>

<u>McGhan Med. Corp., 184 F.3d 1300, 1306 (11th Cir. 1999)</u>. Summary judgment is proper when "there

is no genuine issue as to any material fact and . . . the moving party is entitled to a judgment as a matter of law."

Fed.R.Civ.P. 56(c).

Two elements must be proven in order to establish a prima facie claim for copyright infringement: (1) that Calhoun owns a valid copyright in "Before His Eyes," and (2) that McGee copied "constituent elements of the copyrighted work that are original." Feist Publications, Inc. v. Rural Tel.

Serv. Co., 499 U.S. 340, 361 (1991). To establish copying, Calhoun must show that McGee had access to "Before His Eyes," and that "Emmanuel" is so substantially similar to "Before His Eyes" that "an average lay observer would recognize the alleged copy as having been appropriated from the original work."(FN6) Original Appalachian Artworks, Inc. v. Toy Loft, 684 F.2d 821, 829 (11the Cir. 1982) (citation omitted). "Proof of access and substantial similarity raises only a presumption of copying which may be rebutted by [McGee/Assigns] with evidence of independent creation."(FN7) Id. While McGee/Assigns assert that the two simple melodies are not substantially similar, much less strikingly similar, even a casual comparison of the two compositions compels the conclusion that the two compositions are practically identical. Given the limited number of musical notes (as opposed to words in a language), the combination of those notes and their phrasing, it is not surprising that a simple composition of a short length might well be susceptible to original creation by more than one composer.(FN8) However, in the realm of copyright, identical expression does not necessarily constitute infringement.(FN9) Just as two paintings of the same subject in nature may appear identical, the two paintings' origins may be of independent creation.(FN10)

McGee can fully negate any claim of infringement if he can prove that he independently created "Emmanuel." Benson v. Coca Cola Co., 795 F.2d 973, 975 (11th Cir. 1986) (en banc) ("testimony [of writers of allegedly infringing song] constitutes uncontradicted evidence of independent creation, fully negating any claim of infringement"). Once McGee offers evidence of independent creation, Calhoun has the burden of proving that McGee in fact copied "Before His Eyes." Miller v. Universal City Studios, Inc., 650 F.2d 1365, 1375 (5th Cir. 1981).

As the district court points out, McGee stated in his affidavit that he "independently created 'Emmanuel' during [a] church service in May or June 1976. [He] did not use any pre-existing material as a basis for the song. [He] did not use any sheet music, lead sheets or hymnals." R3-116-21. Moreover, McGee provided affidavits of several witnesses who corroborate his independent creation of "Emmanuel" during a church service. R3-69-2. Calhoun did not offer any evidence to contradict McGee's testimony. Therefore, the district court was correct in concluding that "McGee's testimony constitutes uncontradicted evidence of independent creation, which fully negates any claim of infringement." R3-116-22.

Furthermore, the district court found that "Emmanuel" was independently created by McGee because he had no access or reasonable opportunity(FN11) to view "Before His Eyes." Calhoun provides three theories to attempt to establish McGee had access to view "Before His Eyes." First, Calhoun alleges that he taught students from the state of Washington while he was an instructor at the Stamps-Blackwood School of Gospel Music in Kentucky, and that these students procured and made his music available to McGee. R3-116-6. Calhoun provided seven names and addresses of students from the state of Washington that he taught in the summers from 1972 to 1976. The district court noted that Calhoun did not indicate whether these seven students resided in Washington during the time period of 1972 to 1976, when he allegedly taught them. Furthermore, Calhoun did not offer any affidavits of these seven individuals to corroborate his allegations that they provided his music to McGee or anyone associated with the King's Temple Church. Nor did Calhoun proffer any evidence to rebut McGee's affidavits or declarations stating that he created "Emmanuel" without any sheet music or lead sheets. McGee wrote "Emmanuel" during a church service at the King's Temple Church in Seattle, Washington in the presence of eye witnesses who corroborate McGee's independent creation of the song. R3-69-2, ¶ 2.

Calhoun also argues that McGee heard "Before His Eyes" on the radio, television, or at a performance. He performed "Before His Eyes" on television three times. However, Calhoun offered no admissible evidence to show that these performances were aired outside of Atlanta and Portsmouth, Virginia.(FN12) The only evidence offered by Calhoun was a letter from the producer of The 700 Club, where Calhoun performed "Before His Eyes" on 6 October 1972. The letter explained that the The 700 Club was broadcast throughout the South, but, most notably, the letter did not indicate that the show was available in any part of the Pacific Northwest region of the country.

In addition, Calhoun contended that "Before His Eyes" was performed and promoted at concerts, in churches, to record labels, and over the radio, specifically over The Grand Ole Opry Gospel Radio, which was syndicated from Nashville, Tennessee. The only evidence that his song was accessible in the state of Washington was a letter that Calhoun provided from the Operations manager of WSM, the radio station that broadcasts The Grand Ole Opry Gospel Radio, that stated "[r]eception of WSM in Washington state, therefore, while possible from time to time, is not likely to have occurred in the 1970s on anything resembling a consistent basis." R3-116-8. Furthermore, Calhoun provided no evidence to refute McGee's testimony that he had "never seen nor heard the television program 'Warner Robbins Presents,' . . . never seen the television program 'The 700 Club,'" nor had he "heard the radio program 'The Grand Ole' Opry Gospel Hour.'" Id. at 8-9

As the district court points out, the evidence does not support Calhoun's claim that "Before His Eyes" received widespread publicity. Calhoun has only received $11 in performing rights and publishing royalties for "Before His Eyes." Furthermore, Calhoun has no records of any royalties received from the sale of his album "It's Through Our Faith," on which "Before His Eyes" appears.

Finally, Calhoun asserted that McGee had access to his work because he sent "Before His Eyes" to Faith Music Company, which Lillenas Publishing Company purchased around 1975. Calhoun argued that McGee had dealings with Lillenas, and that Lillenas' alleged possession of his song is sufficient to establish access.

The district court found and the record supports that there was no connection between McGee and Lillenas.

Calhoun did not offer any evidence to rebut McGee's statement that he "never had any relationship with any music publishers" prior to 1976. R3- 116-13. Therefore, Calhoun cannot prove access based on this theory either. Thus, citing no evidentiary basis for access and acknowledging a strong and unrefuted evidentiary basis for McGee's claim of independent creation, the district court did not err in entering judgment against Calhoun.

III. CONCLUSION

These consolidated cases involve the appeal of a grant of summary judgment in which the district court held that there was insufficient evidence to show that "Emmanuel" was strikingly similar to "Before His Eyes," and therefore, Calhoun had no claim for copyright infringement. We conclude that there is no genuine issue of material fact about McGee independently creating "Emmanuel." Therefore, we AFFIRM the judgment of the district court, and conclude that Calhoun's claims of copyright infringement should be barred by McGee's bonafide claim of independent creation.

Notes:

(FN1). The district court granted Calhoun's motion to dismiss Zondervan Publishing House from the action. Additionally, the court granted Lillenas permission to add C.A. Music, Inc. as a third- party defendant.

(FN2). We may affirm the district court on different grounds as long as "the judgment entered is correct on any legal ground regardless of the grounds addressed, adopted or rejected by the district court." Ochran v. United States, 273 F.3d 1315, 1318 (11th Cir. 2001) (citation omitted).

(FN3). It should be emphasized that independent creation is not an affirmative defense (i.e., a claim extraneous to the plaintiff's prima facie case). Rather, independent creation attempts to prove the opposite of the Calhoun's primary claim, i.e., copying by McGee. Keeler Brass Co. v. Continental Brass Co., 862 F.2d 1063, 1066 (4th Cir. 1988).

(FN4). He distributed publication of his musical work in 1970 and inserted and inscribed the copyright notice to the distributed publication in accordance with the Copyright Act of 1909, § 19.

Calhoun eventually filed for registration for his claim of copyright in "Before His Eyes" in 1990.

(FN5). The King's Temple Church is now the New Beginnings Church.

(FN6). Where a plaintiff cannot demonstrate access, he may, nonetheless, establish copying by demonstrating that his original work and the putative infringing work are strikingly similar. Seea Herzog v. Castle Rock Entertainment, 193 F.3d 1241, 1249 (11th Cir. 1999); Benson v. Coca Cola Co., 795 F.2d 973, 975 n.2 (11th Cir. 1986) (en banc); Ferguson v. National Broadcasting Co., 584 F.2d 111, 113 (5th Cir. 1978).

(FN7). Music is often the milieu in which the copyright concepts of "strikingly similar" and "independent creation" have been involved. See Selle v. Gibb, 741 F.2d 896 (7th Cir. 1984) (plaintiff failed to show that musical group Bee Gees had access to plaintiff's song "Let It End" before they composed "How Deep Is Your Love"); Benson, 795 F.2d at 975 (song "I'd Like to Buy the World a Coke" was an independent creation and did not infringe copyright of song "Don't Cha Know");Repp & K& R Music, Inc. v. Webber, 132 F.3d 822 (2nd Cir. 1997) (song "Till You" did not infringe copyright for song "Close Every Door"); Tisi v. Patrick, 97 F. Supp 2d 539 (S.D.N.Y. 2000) (composer failed to show (1) that performer had access to "Sell Your Soul" and (2) the necessary "striking similarity" between "Sell Your Soul" and "Take a Picture").

(FN8). This is particularly true in certain genres of music where familiar phrasing is present. Here the genre is church music. We are only dealing with a basic melody - not lyrics or harmonic background or accompaniment- here, only a short melody is at issue.

(FN9). We have cautioned trial courts in this circuit "not to be swayed by the fact that two works embody similar or even identical ideas." Toy Loft, 684 F.2d at 829 n. 11. See also MiTek Holdings, Inc. v. Arce Engineering Company, Inc., 89 F.3d 1548 (11th Cir. 1996) (competitor's copying of protectable elements of copyrighted computer programs was de minimis and not actionable); Bateman v. Mnemonics, Inc., 79 F.3d 1532 (11th Cir. 1996).

(FN10). Franklin Mint Corp. v. National Wildlife Art Exchange, Inc., 575 F.2d 62 (3rd Cir. 1978) (while ideas in the two paintings of cardinals involved were similar, the expressions were not, and thus, no copyright infringement); See also Leigh v. Warner Bros., 212 F.3d 1210, 1214 (11th Cir. 2000) (photographs of the same sculpture portraying the figure in the same pose, alone, did not give rise to infringement); Concrete Machinery Co., Inc. v. Classic Lawn Ornaments, Inc., 843 F.2d 600 (1st Cir. 1988); Selle, 741 F.2d at 896 (stating that "two works may be identical in every detail, but, if the alleged infringer created the accused work independently or both works were copied from a common source in the public domain, then there is no infringement"); Herbert Rosenthal Jewerly Corp. v.

Kalpakian, 446 F.2d 738 (9th Cir. 1971) (copying of expression was not barred where "idea" of a jeweled bee pin and the "expression" of the "idea" were inseparable); 3 Nimmer, § 13.03[B][2][b] ("if the only original aspect of a work lies in its literal expression, then only a very close similarity, verging on the identical, will suffice to constitute an infringing copy.").

(FN11). Since evidence of actual viewing or knowledge of the copyrighted work is virtually impossible to prove, we regard access as a "reasonable opportunity to view" the copyrighted work. Herzog v. Castle Rock Entertainment, 193 F.3d 1241, 1249 (11th Cir. 1999).

(FN12). Calhoun stated in a deposition that he did not know what television station were affiliates of the CBN network during the time of his performances.

BIRCH, Circuit Judge, specially concurring:

I concur. Moreover, because the confluence of facts in this case presents a "perfect storm," I think it enticing, if not necessary, to address an alternative basis upon which the district court's judgment could be sustained- - - unreasonable delay. Whether unreasonable delay may bar a claim of copyright infringement(FN1)where there is considerable delay in filing suit and a bona fide claim of independent creation exists is globally one of first impression and merits examination. I am persuaded that just as equitable tolling(FN2) may save an otherwise tardy infringement action; unreasonable delay should bar such an action where a bonafide independent creation claim is presented.(FN3)

I conclude that the challenging author must not unreasonably delay in his assertion of copyright as to the other author's work where he seeks to have a judicial determination of the challenged author's originality of creation.(FN4)

Failing to do so would constitute a manifest injustice and potentially unjust denial of the challenged author's constitutionally guaranteed copyright in his original (albeit later) work. The gravamen of Calhoun's lawsuit is that he claims ownership in "Emmanuel" because he contends the melodies are practically identical. I conclude that this claim and all those logically following therefrom should be barred, including any infringement claims. Such an approach is not without precedent or logic.(FN5)

1. Period of Delay

The statute of limitations for copyright infringement claims is triggered by violations, that is, actual infringements. The limitations period may be triggered when a plaintiff knows or, in the exercise of reasonable diligence, should have known about an infringement. 17 U.S.C. § 507(b). One should look to the appropriate statute of limitations as a guide to determine whether the delay was reasonable. Kason Indus., Inc., 120 F.3d at 1203.

The Copyright Act sets forth a three-year statute of limitations for claims of copyright infringement. 17 U.S.C. § 507(b). Accordingly, one basis for determining whether Calhoun's delay in filing suit was reasonable is the three-year statute of limitations in § 507(b).

Calhoun's period of delay ranges anywhere from 23 years, from the time that "Emmanuel" was written in 1976, to 13 years, from the time it was licensed to churches around the world in 1984. During this time Calhoun took no legal action to stop or to seek redress for the putative infringement. By any calculation, this delay is more than enough. See Freedom Savings and Loan Ass'n. v. Way, 757 F.2d 1176, 1186 fn. 8 (11th Cir.

1986) (five years delay in filing trademark infringement suit considered sufficient); Studiengesellschaft Kohle mbH v. Eastman Kodak Co., 616 F.2d 1315, 1326 (5th Cir. 1980) (delay presumed unreasonable when exceeded the statutory six-year period). Applying the three-year benchmark, it is clear that Calhoun's delay of over a decade plainly constitutes a significant delay.

2. Inexcusable Delay

Next, the cause of the delay should be examined to determine whether Calhoun's lengthy delay in filing suit was excusable. Kason, 120 F.3d at 1204. Some examples of permissible delay, frequently viewed in the context of equitable tolling, among other circuits include: (1) the need for the exhaustion of remedies through the administrative process, Couveau v. American Airlines, Inc., 218 F.3d 1078, 1083-84 (9th Cir. 2000); (2) additional time to determine whether the scope of the proposed infringement will justify the cost of litigation, ," Lotus Dev. Corp. v.

Borland Int'l, Inc., 831 F.Supp. 202, 219 (D.Mass.1993), rev'd on other grounds, 49 F.3d 807

(1st Cir.1995); and (3) the need for additional time to evaluate the extent of the infringement, A.C. Aukerman Co. v. R.L. Chaides Constr. Co., 960 F.2d 1020, 1033 (Fed. Cir. 1992).

To explain his delay in filing suit, Calhoun claims that he was unaware that "Emmanuel" existed. McGee/Asignees contend that the delay was inexcusable because Calhoun should have known about his alleged claim of infringement well before 1997, the date he claims to have "discovered" the putatively infringing and strikingly similar composition, due to the popularity of "Emmanuel" throughout the past two decades. "Emmanuel" has appeared in a number of major Christian denominational hymnals and has been translated into dozens of foreign languages. It has consistently been ranked in the top twenty requested Christian songs. Calhoun worked as both a choir director and an organist for almost ten years prior to filing suit, and regularly played songs from hymnals that contained the chorus "Emmanuel." Furthermore, Calhoun, himself, listed over 21 publications that included "Emmanuel" in addition to the list of 20 publications submitted by McGee/Assignees during discovery. R1-43; R2-47, 48.

The district court found "it difficult to believe that [Calhoun] did not have notice of the allegedly infringing song prior to 1997. [H]ad [Calhoun] exercised an iota of diligence, he would have learned of the possible infringement earlier." R3-108 at 8. I agree. Given the evidence in this record no reasonable juror could have concluded that Calhoun exercised any diligence in protecting his copyright. With copyright rights come concomitant responsibilities, including the responsibility to assert those rights in a timely manner after exercise of diligence. Moreover, in the district court Calhoun argued that the two compositions were strikingly similar in melody (as opposed to lyrics), thus compelling a recognition of the putative infringement.

Given the length of time that had passed, the wide dissemination of "Emmanuel," and his substantial experience and involvement with church music, Calhoun should have known about "Emmanuel," and therefore, the delay in filing suit was inexcusable.

3. Prejudice

The final factor informing the decision to bar by unreasonable delay is whether McGee/Assigns have been prejudiced by Calhoun's delay. In similar contexts courts have recognized a variety of factors that constitute prejudice: (1) important witnesses have died; (2) the memories of witnesses have been dulled; (3) relevant records have been destroyed or are missing; and (4) the loss of monetary investments which likely would have been prevented by earlier suit. Eastman Kodak Co., 616 F.2d at 1326. See Jackson v. Axton, 25 F.3d 884 (9th Cir. 1994); Byron v. Chevrolet Motor Div. of General Motors Corp. 1995 WL 465130 (S.D.N.Y. 1995). Cf. Hoste v. Radio Corporation of America, 654 F.2d 11 (6th Cir. 1981). Calhoun admits that the song "Emmanuel" may not have become as widespread as it is today had he objected sooner. As McGee/Assigns point out, since 1984,

C.A. Music has licensed "Emmanuel" to hundreds of licensees, 28 of whom make up the assigns in this case. McGee's assigns have invested a substantial amount of time and money in the licensing of

"Emmanuel" by relying on the validity of its copyright. Accordingly, McGee/Assigns are able to demonstrate prejudice by showing that they suffered consequences that they would not have, had Calhoun acted promptly.

While the foregoing analysis is not required for a resolution of this dispute, perhaps my rumination may be useful to those confronted with this intriguing copyright scenario in the future.

Notes:

(FN1). Heretofore, courts have frequently considered delay in initiating an action where, as is typical, preliminary injunctive relief has been requested. Essentially, where unreasonable delay has occurred, courts have concluded that such delay is suggestive of a lack of irreparable harm. See, e.g., Richard Feiner and Co., Inc. v. Turner Entertainment Co., MGM/UA, 98 F.3d 33 (2nd Cir. 1996); Tom Doherty Associates, Inc. v. Saban Entertainment 60 F.3d 27 (2d Cir. 1995); Forry, Inc. v. Neundorfer, Inc., 837 F.2d 259 (6th Cir. 1988); Markowitz Jewerly Co., Inc. v.

Chapal/Zenray, Inc., 988 F. Supp. 404 (S.D.N.Y. 1997); Fritz v. Arthur D. Little, Inc., 944 F.Supp. 95, 98 (D.Mass.1996).

(FN2). See Stone v. Williams, 970 F.2d 1043 (2d Cir. 1992); Taylor Meirick, 712 F.2d 112 (7th Cir. 1983); Prather v. Neva Paperbacks, Inc., 446 F.2d 338 (5th Cir. 1971); 3 Nimmer § 12.05[B].

(FN3). I stress that here I am not applying a laches analysis to an infringement action. Rather I analyze this unique case as essentially a declaratory judgment action, focusing on a musical composition that the first composer in time claims to be identical to the second composer's score when a bona fide claim of independent creation is asserted. The cases, heretofore existing, closest to this unusual case involve claims of putative co-authorship where one of the co- authors seeks a declaration of sole ownership. Thus, my approach is closest to that taken by the Second Circuit in Merchant v. Levy, 92 F.3d 51, 57 n.8 (2d Cir. 1996) (a co-authorship case where laches was not addressed, but a delay bar was imposed).

Moreover, this avoids the need to embrace one side or the other in applying the laches defense.

The circuits are split on whether it is appropriate to consider a laches defense where an infringement action is brought within the statutory three- year period of limitations. See Stone v. Williams, 970 F.2d 1043, 1048 (2d Cir. 1992) (where uncertainty surrounded the relative's status of the author's family, the statute of limitations was not applied to defeat the copyright co- ownership claim of an author's relative accruing more than three years before the lawsuit); Lyons Partnership v. Morris Costumes, Inc., 243 F.3d 789, 797 (4th Cir. 2001) ("in connection with copyright claims, separation of powers principles dictate that an equitable timeliness rule adopted by courts cannot bar claims that are brought within the legislatively prescribed statute of limitations"); Danjaq LLC v. Sony Corporation, 263 F.3d 942, 954 (9th Cir. 2001) ("If a defendant can show harm from the delay, the court may, in extraordinary circumstances, defeat the claim based on laches, though the claim is within the analogous limitations period")(citation omitted). Perhaps the Court's opinion in Nat'l Railroad Passenger Corp. v. Morgan, 122 S. Ct. 2061, 2077, U.S. (2002) will clarify that issue.

(FN4). A work is "original," and therefore accorded copyright protection, if it is independently created by the author and possesses some minimal degree of creativity. 17 U.S.C. § 101 et seq.

(FN5). See, e.g., Merchant, 92 F.3d at 56 ("[w]e hold that plaintiffs claiming to be co-authors are time-barred three years after accrual of their claim from seeking a declaration of copyright co-ownership rights and remedies that would flow from such a declaration."); Danjaq LLC, 263 F.3d at 954 (upholding a district court's application of laches to prevent a plaintiff from pursuing copyright infringement claims when plaintiff filed suit "at least twenty-one years--and more likely, thirty-six years" after having knowledge of the potential claims); Margo v. Weiss, 213 F.3d 55, 60-61 (2nd Cir. 2000); Zuill v. Shanahan, 80 F.3d 1366, 1371 (9th Cir.

1996) (barring "a declaratory judgment of co-ownership and the relief ancillary to such a claim"); New Era Publications Int'l v. Henry Holt & Co., 873 F.2d 576, 584-85 (2d Cir.1989) (laches barred plaintiff from enjoining publication of author's biography when plaintiff had delayed "unreasonabl[y] and inexcusabl[y]" in filing suit.); Fort Knox Music, Inc. v. Baptiste, 47 F. Supp 2d 481, 483-84 (S.D.N.Y. 1999); 3 Nimmer § 12.05 [c], n.63 ("If A cannot

be heard to claim belatedly that he co-authored a work with B 20 years ago, which would result in A owning 50% of the copyright, then all the more so C must be barred from belatedly claiming that she solely authored a work on which D has been claiming authorship credit for 20 years, which would result in C owning 100% of the copyright").

CASE SUMMARY

(PAGES 75-83)

Joel Songs v. Shelley Broadcasting Company (2007) - Radio stations infringed on songwriter's copyrights by not paying license fees. The station owners argued that they did not believe they needed to pay license fees because the content was broadcast during satellite programming. The stations were ordered to pay $5k per violation and permanent injunction (requiring the defendant to refrain from playing ASCAP members' copyrighted songs) was imposed against the station owner (in light of past copyright violations).

Note: This case illustrates the potential liability of station owners for contributory infringement. The owner, while not directly involved, was also at fault for not adequately supervising his station's content. This risk is also present where unsupervised technology departments and broadcast providers fail to supervise worship service content.

CASE LAW

491 F.Supp.2d 1080

JOELSONGS, et al., Plaintiffs, v.

SHELLEY BROADCASTING COMPANY, INC., et al., Defendants.

Civil Action No. 1:06cv774-MHT.

United States District Court, M.D. Alabama, Southern Division. June 8, 2007.

Page 1081

COPYRIGHT MATERIAL OMITTED

Page 1082

Dylan Cook Black, James William Gewin, Bradley Arant Rose & White LLP, Birmingham, AL, for Plaintiffs.

Steve G. McGowan, Steve McGowan LLC, Dothan, AL, for Defendants.

OPINION

MYRON H. THOMPSON, District Judge.

The plaintiffs are members of the American Society of Composers, Authors and Publishers

("ASCAP"), to which they have granted a non-exclusive right to license non-dramatic public performances of their copyrighted musical compositions.[1] The plaintiffs brought this lawsuit against defendants Shelly Broadcasting Company, Inc., Stage Door Development, Inc., and H. Jack Mizell, charging that they violated the Copyright Act, 17 U.S.C. §§ 101-1332, by playing ASCAP's copyrighted musical compositions on the radio without authorization. This court has jurisdiction under 28 U.S.C. § 1338(a) (copyright) and § 1331 (federal question).

Currently before the court is the plaintiffs' motion for summary judgment. The motion will be granted.

I. SUMMARY-JUDGMENT STANDARD

Summary judgment is appropriate "if the pleadings, depositions, answers to interrogatories, and admissions on file, together with the affidavits, if any, show that there is no genuine issue as to any material fact and that the moving party is entitled to a judgment as a matter of law." Fed.R.Civ.P. 56(c). Under Rule 56, the party seeking summary judgment must first inform the court of the basis for the motion, and the burden then shifts to the non-moving party to demonstrate why summary judgment would not be proper. *Celotex Corp. v. Catrett,* 477 U.S. 317, 323, 106 S.Ct.2548, 91 L.Ed.2d 265 (1986); *see also Fitzpatrick v. City of Atlanta,* 2 F.3d 1112, 1115-17 (11th Cir.1993) (discussing burden-shifting under Rule 56).

The court's role at the summary-judgment stage is not to weigh the evidence or to determine the truth of the matter, but rather to determine only whether a genuine issue exists for trial. *Anderson v. Liberty Lobby, Inc.,* 477 U.S. 242, 249, 106 S.Ct. 2505, 91 L.Ed.2d 202 (1986). In doing so, the court must view the evidence in the light most favorable to the nonmoving party and draw all reasonable inferences in favor of that party. *Matsushita Elec.*

Indus. Co. v. Zenith Radio Corp., 475 U.S. 574, 587, 106 S.Ct. 1348, 89 L.Ed.2d 538 (1986).

II. FACTS

On February 25 and 27, 2006, several ASCAP copyrighted compositions were broadcast over radio-station WGEA, which is operated by Shelley Broadcasting. On Page 1083

February 24, 25, and 26, 2006, additional selections of ASCAP copyrighted songs were broadcast on radio-station WRJMFM, which is operated by Stage Door. Mizell is the owner of Shelley Broadcasting and Stage Door. A total of 20 ASCAP-copyrighted songs were broadcast over the defendants' radio stations. Neither station had ASCAP's permission to perform these compositions.

The 20 broadcasted songs are "We Didn't Start The Fire," "Little Wing," "Hey There," "Begin The Beguine," "Pink Houses," "Panama," "This Will Be (An Everlasting Love)," "Raspberry Beret," "Faith," "Master Of Puppets," "Little Red Corvette," "Light My Fire," "Big Yellow Taxi," "Jump," "Rikki, Don't Lose That Number," "God Will Make A Way," "Since I Don't Have You," "We Have Come Into His House (To Worship Him)," "Small Town," and "1999."

III. DISCUSSION

"To establish a prima-facie copyright infringement case for a musical composition, a plaintiff may prove

(1) ownership of a valid copyright and (2) public performance' of the copyrighted work without authorization." *Simpleville Music v. Mizell,* 451 F.Supp.2d 1293, 1295 (M.D.Ala.2006) (Thompson, J.) (citing 17 U.S.C. § 106(4) (subject to specific exclusions outlined in the Copyright Act, "the owner of copyright ... has the exclusive rights ... in the case of ... musical ... works to perform the copyrighted work publicly")); *cf.* *Feist Publications, Inc. v. Rural Telephone Service Co., Inc.* 499 U.S. 340, 361, 111 S.Ct. 1282, 113 L.Ed.2d 358 (1991) ("To establish infringement, two elements must be proven: (1) ownership of a valid copyright, and (2) copying of constituent elements of the work that are original.").

The plaintiffs have satisfied the first element by submitting copies of the copyright-registration certificates which, pursuant to 17 U.S.C. § 410(c), constitute prima-facie evidence of copyright ownership. 17 U.S.C. § 410(c) ("In any judicial proceedings the certificate of a registration made before or within five years after first publication of the work shall constitute prima facie evidence of the validity of the copyright and of the facts stated in the certificate."); *see also Simpleville*

*Music,*https://apps.fastcase.com/Research/Pages/Document.aspx?L TID=gg MxPz7l2Gu%2bzY%2bETZFHYKEtiQby%2f0Sugj%2b Wwb5OAZpJVs6 Uth2jlNuC%2fv9wax%2fWjGcdISsdUX4Fyv QoXiDD8oJU1y%2bXxmBI escKukze4t0ffZ9JvfrUfc7nLVe5vM iz&ECF=451+F.Supp.2d+at+1296 451 F.Supp.2d at 1296 ("The plaintiffs have satisfied the first element by submitting copies of the copyright registration certificates.").

In satisfaction of the second element, the plaintiffs present the affidavits of Jerry Glaze, who recorded the broadcasts off radio- stations WGEA and WRJM-FM on the days in dispute, and Oleksander Kuzyszyn, who listened to the tapes and identified that the 20 compositions constituting the basis of this lawsuit were found on the tape recordings. By failing to respond to the plaintiffs' request for admissions, the defendants admitted to the songs being played, *see* Fed.R.Civ.P. 36(a), and the defendants also admit that they did not have permission to broadcast the 20 songs.

The defendants, however, assert three defenses to the copyright claims: that (1) the music was played as part of satellite programming for which they did not need a license; (2) only the radio stations, not Mizell, should be liable for the alleged infringements; and (3) they did not intend to violate copyright laws. The court will discuss the validity of each defense.

A. Songs Played During Satellite Programming

The defendants contend that all the songs were played during satellite programming and that the satellite companies assured Mizell that no copyrighted material would be played. Although the Page 1084 defendants have not presented any physical evidence to support this contention, the assurances, even if made, do not absolve the defendants of liability because "a broadcaster who is aware of his obligations under copyright law remains responsible for ensuring that copyrighted music is not aired without permission." *Jobete Music Co., Inc. v. Johnson*

Communications, Inc., 285 F.Supp.2d 1077, 1089 (S.D.Ohio 2003) (Rice, C. J.); *see also Simpleville Music,*https://apps.fastcase.com/Research/Pages/Document.aspx?L TID=gg MxPz7l2Gu%2bzY%2bETZFHYKEtiQby%2f0Sugj%2b Wwb5OAZpJVs6 Uth2jlNuC%2fv9wax%2fWjGcdISsdUX4Fyv QoXiDD8oJU1y%2bXxmBI escKukze4t0ffZ9JvfrUfc7nLVe5vM iz&ECF=451+F.Supp.2d+at+1299 451 F.Supp.2d at 1299 ("Although Mizell did not produce the commercial or the radio shows himself, he was still responsible for ensuring that all of the licensing fees were paid. Consequently, Mizell's no-intent defense is meritless."). Therefore, although the copyrighted music was aired through satellite programming, the defendants were still responsible for ensuring that all of the licensing fees were paid; the defendants are still liable for violating the Copyright Act.

B. Intent

The defendants protest that they did not intend to play copyrighted material and took measures to protect against such infringements. However, "intention to infringe is not essential under the [Copyright] Act." *Buck v.*

Jewell-LaSalle Realty Co., 283 U.S. 191, 198, 51 S.Ct. 410, 75 L.Ed. 971 (1931); *see also Simpleville Music,*https://apps.fastcase.com /Research/Pages/Document.aspx?LTID=gg MxPz7l2Gu%2bzY%2 bETZFHYKEtiQby%2f0Sugj%2bWwb5OAZpJVs6 Uth2jlNuC% 2fv9wax%2fWjGcdISsdUX4FyvQoXiDD8oJU1y%2bXx mBI escKukze4t0ffZ9JvfrUfc7nLVe5vMiz&ECF=451+F.Sup p.2d+at+ 1299 451 F.Supp.2d at 1299; 4 Melville B. Nimmer & David Nimmer, Nimmer on Copyright § 13.08 (2006) ("In actions for statutory copyright infringement, the innocent intent of the defendant will not constitute a defense to a finding of liability."). The defendants' lack of intent does not shield them from liability.

C. Personal Liability of Owner

Mizell denies liability on the ground that he did not personally participate in, or profit from, the infringement; he says he performed his duties as only the owner. However, the record is clear that, as the president, owner, and sole stockholder of the companies that own WGEA and WRJM- FM, he was essentially a one-man show. A person, "including a corporate officer, who has the ability to supervise infringing activity and has a financial interest in that activity, or who personally participates in that activity is personally liable for the infringement." *Southern Bell. Tel. & Tel. Co. v. Associated Tel. Directory Publishers,* 756 F.2d 801, 811 (11th Cir.1985) (citation omitted). Similarly, "under the Copyright Act, an individual who is the dominant influence in a corporation, and through his position can control the acts of that corporation, may be held jointly and severally liable with the corporate entity for copyright infringements, even in the absence of the individual's actual knowledge of the infringements." *Simpleville*

*Music,*https://apps.fastcase.com/Research/Pages/Document.aspx?L TID=gg MxPz7l2Gu%2bzY%2bETZFHYKEtiQby%2f0Sugj%2b

Wwb5OAZpJVs6
Uth2jlNuC%2fv9wax%2fWjGcdISsdUX4Fyv
QoXiDD8oJU1y%2bXxmBI
escKukze4t0ffZ9JvfrUfc7nLVe5v
Miz&ECF=451+F.Supp.2d+at+1299 451 F.Supp.2d at 1299 (quoting *Quartet Music v. Kissimmee Broadcasting, Inc.*, 795 F.Supp. 1100, 1103 (M.D.Fl.1992)) (Kellam, J.). "The record is clear that Mizell fits the bill of being the supervising, dominant figure at the two radio stations." *Id.* As such, he is personally liable for the Copyright Act violations.

D. Damages

17 U.S.C. § 504(c) of the Copyright Act allows a plaintiff to recover "statutory damages" in lieu of actual damages.[2]

Page 1085

The court without finding willfulness can award up to $ 30,000 per infringement in statutory damages. *Id.* A finding of willfulness allows the court to raise the statutory award to no more than $ 100,000 per infringement. *Id.* The plaintiffs are seeking $ 5,000 in statutory damages per infringement. Because plaintiffs are seeking less than $ 30,000, willfulness on the part of the defendants is not required. However, the record shows that the defendants did willfully infringe on the plaintiffs' copyrights.

The defendants argue that they did not willfully violate the Copyright Act because the alleged infringement occurred prior to the resolution of *Simpleville Music,* where this court found that the same defendants had infringed other ASCAP-member plaintiffs' copyrights; the defendants contend that up until that point they did not know that they were violating the Copyright Act. However, the record indicates, and the defendants do not dispute, that before this or any other lawsuit was filed against them, ASCAP repeatedly offered them an ASCAP license, which would have permitted them to play the plaintiffs' copyrighted works legally. ASCAP further informed the defendants that, without a proper license, their conduct would violate copyright laws. Nevertheless, the defendants refused ASCAP's offers of a license, while continuing to broadcast copyrighted songs.

Moreover, in 1993, in *Bencap v. Shelley Broadcasting,* civil action no.

93-A-696-S (M.D.Ala. Dec. 28, 1993), Shelley Broadcasting and Mizell agreed to a consent judgment where they admitted to "willfully" infringing the copyrights of the ASCAP-member plaintiffs, and they were permanently enjoined from publicly performing the plaintiffs' musical compositions in the future. And, in 2004, in *Simpleville Music,* before entry of a final judgment against Mizell in that case and before the infringements in the instant case, this court entered a default judgment in the amount of $ 48,000 against Shelley Broadcasting and Stage Door for infringing the copyrights of the ASCAP-member plaintiffs in that case.

In light of the defendants' previous, continuous, and knowing and willful infringements of ASCAP-members' copyrights, it is indisputable that their violations of the Copyright Act here were willful. However, the court does not find it appropriate to increase the statutory damages above the amount requested by the plaintiffs; the court will award statutory damages in the amount of $ 5,000 per violation.

E. Injunction

The plaintiffs also seek, pursuant to § 502 of the Copyright Act, to enjoin the defendants from publicly performing ASCAP members' copyrighted music. Section 502(a) of the Copyright Act specifically authorizes this court to "grant ... final injunctions on such terms as it may deem reasonable to prevent or restrain infringement of a copyright." *See Pacific & Southern Co., Inc. v. Duncan,* 744 F.2d 1490, 1499 n. 17 (11th Cir.1984) (the Copyright Act authorizes an injunction "on such terms as it may deem reasonable to prevent or restrain infringement of a copyright"),

Page 1086

cert. denied, https://apps.fastcase.com/Research/Pages/Document.aspx?LTID=ggMxPz7l2Gu%2bzY%2bETZFHYKEtiQby%2f0Sugj%2bWwb5OAZpJVs6Uth2jlNuC%2fv9wax%2fWjGcdISsdUX4FyvQoXiDD8oJU1y%2bXxmBIescKukze4t0ffZ9Jvf rUfc7nLVe5vMiz&ECF=471+U.S.+1004 471 U.S. 1004, 105 S.Ct. 1867, 85 L.Ed.2d 161 (1985).

While the court may grant a permanent injunction "on such terms as it may deem reasonable to prevent or restrain infringement of a copyright," 17

U.S.C. § 502(a), that grant is not unlimited; the court may, as a general matter, do so only when there is a substantial likelihood of further infringement of a plaintiff's copyrights. *Simpleville*

*Music,*https://apps.fastcase.com/Research/Pages/Document.aspx?L TID=gg MxPz7l2Gu%2bzY%2bETZFHYKEtiQby%2f0Sugj%2b Wwb5OAZpJVs6 Uth2jlNuC%2fv9wax%2fWjGcdISsdUX4Fyv QoXiDD8oJU1y%2bXxmBI escKukze4t0ffZ9JvfrUfc7nLVe5v Miz&ECF=451+F.Supp.2d+at+1300 451 F.Supp.2d at 1300; *see also* 4 Melville B. Nimmer & David Nimmer, Nimmer on Copyright

§ 14-06[B](2006).

The plaintiffs contend that the defendants are likely to continue infringing on the copyrighted compositions that belong to them and all other ASCAP members as demonstrated by the fact that the defendants have been sued twice already, and yet they have willfully continued to infringe on the copyrights of ASCAP members. As stated, in 1993, in *Bencap,* Shelley Broadcasting and Mizell agreed to a consent judgment where they admitted to "willfully" infringing the copyrights of the ASCAP- member plaintiffs, and they were permanently enjoined from publicly performing the plaintiffs' musical compositions in the future, and, in 2004, in *Simpleville Music,* before the infringements in the instant case, this court entered a default judgment in the amount of $ 48,000 against Shelley Broadcasting and Stage Door for infringing the copyrights of the ASCAP- member plaintiffs in that case. The defendants have, therefore, unsuccessfully defended two prior lawsuits in which money judgments were awarded against them, and yet they continued to violate the Copyright Act by broadcasting copyrighted compositions without first obtaining a proper license. It is indisputable that money judgments have not been an effective tool to "prevent or restrain infringement[s] of ... copyright[s]," 17 U.S.C.

§ 502(a), by the defendants.

The court recognizes that the injunction the plaintiffs seek goes beyond a prohibition of the unauthorized broadcasting of the plaintiffs' songs only. The court nevertheless considers such a broad injunction warranted for several reasons. First, the defendants have not objected to the breadth of the injunction. Second, while it would appear that this lawsuit is brought by the named plaintiffs, it is really brought by ASCAP as the enforcement organization on behalf of the named plaintiffs. ASCAP is "a clearing house for copyright owners and users" that facilitates the negotiation of licenses and the monitoring and enforcement of infringements where it would be impractical for individual copyright owners to do so on their own. *Broadcast Music, Inc. v. Columbia Broadcasting System, Inc.* 441 U.S. 1, 5, 99 S.Ct. 1551, 60 L.Ed.2d 1 (1979). "[I]ts ... members grant it nonexclusive rights to license non- dramatic performances of their works," *id.,* and the license includes "the ... enforcement against unauthorized copyright use." *Id.* at 20, 99 S.Ct. 1551. Therefore, it is ASCAP, acting through its members, that is asking for the broad injunction here. Third, there is substantial and longstanding precedent for such broad injunctions in circumstances similar to those presented here. *See, e.g.,* *Harrison Music Corp. v. Tesfaye,* 293 F.Supp.2d 80, 83 (D.D.C.2003) (Leon, J.); *All Nations Music v. Christian Family Network, Inc.,* 989 F.Supp. 863 (W.D.Mich.1997) (Miles, J.); *Cross Keys Publ. Co. v. Wee, Inc.,* 921 F.Supp. 479, 481 (W.D.Mich.1995) (Quist, J.).

Therefore, the plaintiffs are entitled to an injunction prohibiting the defendants from directly or indirectly infringing on Page 1087 the copyright rights of all ASCAP members.

* * * * * *

Because, without question, the plaintiffs have established a prima- facie case of copyright infringement of each of the 20 songs and the defendants have failed to offer valid defenses, summary judgment in favor of the plaintiffs will be entered. The judgment will include an assessment of a $ 5,000 statutory fee for each of the 20 infringements, for a total of $ 100,000.00 (20 × $ 5,000 = $ 100, 000.00), along with appropriate injunctive relief.

JUDGMENT AND INJUNCTION

In accordance with the memorandum opinion entered this date, it is the ODDER, JUDGMENT, and DECREE of the court that:

(1) The motion for summary judgment (Doc. No. 15) filed by plaintiffs Joelsongs; Experience Hendrix, LLC; Richard Adler, d/b/a Lakshmi Puja Music, Ltd.; Judith Coulter, d/b/a J&J Ross, Co.; Janie Coulter Hartbarger d/b/a J&J Ross, Co.; Warner Bros., Inc.; Emi Full Keel Music Co.; Van Halen Music Co.; Chappell & Co., Inc.; Jay's Enterprises, Inc.; Controversy Music; Creeping Death Music; Doors Music Company; Siquomb Publishing Corp.; Universal Studios, Inc.; Integrity's Hosamma Music;Bonnyview Music, Corp.; and Sound III, Inc. (hereinafter "plaintiffs") is granted.

(2) Judgment is entered in favor of the plaintiffs and against defendants Shelly Broadcasting Company, Inc., Stage Door Development, Inc., and H. Jack Mizell (hereinafter "defendants").

(3) The plaintiffs shall have and recover from the defendants the sum of $100,00.00.

(4) The defendants, their officers, agents, servants, employees, and attorneys, and those person in active concert or participation with them who receive actual notice of this injunction and judgment by personal service or otherwise, are each jointly and separately ENJOINED and RESTRAINED from directly or indirectly infringing American Society of Composers, Authors and Publisher ("ASCAP") members' copyright rights under federal or state law, whether now in existence or later created, that are owned or controlled by members of ASCAP or any parent, subsidiary, or affiliate record label of members of ASCAP.

It is further ORDERED that costs are taxed against the defendants, for which execution may issue.

The United States Marshal is DIRECTED to provide for personal service on the defendants of this judgment and injunction and the accompanying opinion.

The clerk of the court is DIRECTED to enter this document on the civil docket as a final judgment pursuant to Rule 58 of the Federal Rules of Civil Procedure.

Notes:

1. The plaintiffs are: Joelsongs; Experience Hendrix, LLC; Richard Adler, d/b/a Lakshmi Puja Music, Ltd.; Judith Coulter, d/b/a J & J Ross, Co.; Janie Coulter Hartbarger d/b/a J & J Ross, Co.; Warner Bros., Inc.; Emi Full Keel Music Co.; Van Halen Music Co.; Chappell & Co., Inc.; Jay's Enterprises, Inc.; Controversy Music; Creeping Death Music; Doors Music Company; Siquomb Publishing Corp.; Universal Studios, Inc.; Integrity's Hosanna Music; Bonnyview Music, Corp.; and Sound III, Inc.
2. In relevant part, § 504(c) provides:

"(1) Except as provided by clause (2) of this subsection, the copyright owner may elect, at any time before final judgment is rendered, to recover, instead of actual damages and profits, an award of statutory damages for all infringements involved in the action, with respect to any one work, ... in a sum of not less than $ 750 or more than $ 30,000 as the court considers just"

"(2) In a case where the copyright owner sustains the burden of proving, and the court finds, that infringement was committed willfully, the court in its discretion may increase the award of statutory damages to a sum of not more than $ 150,000. In a case where the infringer sustains the burden of proving, and the court finds, that such infringer was not aware and had no reason to believe that his or her acts constituted an infringement of copyright, the court in its discretion may reduce the award of statutory damages to a sum of not less than $200."

CASE SUMMARY

(PAGES 85-141)

Religious Technology Center v. Netcom Online Communication Services, Inc. (1995) - Affiliates of the Church of Scientology claimed that a former member of the church infringed on church copyrights by posting excerpts of protected works online. The defendant claimed the excerpts were posted for debate and criticism, and he did not personally profit from the works. The court ruled in favor of the church, finding that the defendant's copying of entire, previously unpublished works and adding very little criticism, weighed against his fair use defense. The defendant's computer and all related documents were seized and all traces of the works were stripped from his hard drive.

923 F.Supp. 1231

RELIGIOUS TECHNOLOGY CENTER, a California non-profit corporation; and Bridge Publications, Inc., a California non-profit corporation, Plaintiffs, v.

NETCOM ON-LINE COMMUNICATION SERVICES, INC., a

Delaware corporation; Dennis Erlich, an individual; and Tom Klemesrud, an individual, dba Clearwood Data Services, Defendants.

No. C-95-20091 RMW.

United States District Court, N.D. California. September 22, 1995.

Page 1232

COPYRIGHT MATERIAL OMITTED

Page 1233

COPYRIGHT MATERIAL OMITTED

Page 1234

COPYRIGHT MATERIAL OMITTED

Page 1235

COPYRIGHT MATERIAL OMITTED

Page 1236

COPYRIGHT MATERIAL OMITTED

Page 1237

Helena K. Kobrin, North Hollywood, CA, Andrew H. Wilson, Wilson, Ryan & Campilongo, San Francisco, CA, Thomas M. Small, Janet A. Kobrin, Small, Larkin & Kiddé, Los Angeles, CA, Elliot J. Abelson, Los Angeles, CA, for Plaintiffs.

Randolf J. Rice, Pillsbury, Madison & Sutro, San Jose, CA, for Defendant Netcom On-Line Communication Services.

Harold J. McElhinny, Carla Oakley, Morrison & Foerster, San Francisco, CA, for Defendant Dennis Erlich.

Page 1238

Daniel Leipold, Hagenbaugh & Murphy, Orange, CA, for Defendant Tom Klemesrud.

ORDER GRANTING IN PART AND DENYING IN PART PLAINTIFFS' APPLICATION FOR A PRELIMINARY INJUNCTION AND DEFENDANT

ERLICH'S MOTION TO DISSOLVE THE TRO; DENYING PLAINTIFFS' APPLICATION TO EXPAND THE TRO; DENYING PLAINTIFFS' MOTION FOR CONTEMPT; GRANTING ERLICH'S MOTION TO VACATE THE WRIT OF SEIZURE; AND DENYING PLAINTIFFS' REQUEST FOR SANCTIONS AGAINST

ERLICH'S COUNSEL WHYTE, District Judge.

This case involves the scope of intellectual property rights on the Internet.[1] Plaintiffs, two Scientology-affiliated organizations claiming copyright and trade secret protection for the writings of the Church's founder, L. Ron Hubbard, brought this suit against defendant Dennis Erlich ("Erlich"), a former Scientology minister turned vocal critic of the Church, who allegedly put plaintiffs' protected works onto the Internet.[2]

On June 23, 1995, this court heard the parties' arguments on eight motions, five of which relate to Erlich and are discussed herein: (1) plaintiffs' motion for a preliminary injunction against Erlich and Erlich's related motion to dissolve or amend the Amended TRO; (2) plaintiffs' application to expand the TRO; (3)

plaintiffs' motion for contempt against Erlich; (4) Erlich's motion to vacate the writ of seizure; and (5) and plaintiffs' request for sanctions against Erlich's counsel.[3] For the reasons set forth below, the court grants in part and denies in part plaintiffs' motion for a preliminary injunction against Erlich and Erlich's motion to dissolve the TRO, denies plaintiffs' application to expand the TRO, denies plaintiffs' motion for contempt against Erlich, grants Erlich's motion to vacate the writ of seizure, and denies plaintiffs' request for sanctions against Erlich's counsel.

I. BACKGROUND

Defendant Dennis Erlich was a member of the Church of Scientology ("the Church")[4]

Page 1239 from approximately 1968 until 1982. During his years with the Church, Erlich received training to enable him to provide ministerial counseling services, known as "auditing." While with the Church, Erlich had access to various Scientology writings, including those of the Church's founder, L. Ron Hubbard ("Hubbard"), which the Church alleges include published literary works as well as unpublished confidential materials (the "Advanced Technology works"). According to plaintiffs, Erlich had agreed to maintain the confidentiality of the Advanced Technology works.

Since leaving the Church, Erlich has been a vocal critic of Scientology and he now considers it part of his calling to foster critical debate about Scientology through humorous and critical writings. Erlich has expressed his views about the Church by contributing to the Internet "Usenet news- group"[5] called "alt.religion.scientology" ("the newsgroup"), which is an on- line forum for the discussion of issues related to Scientology.[6]

Plaintiffs allege that in the six months prior to their filing suit, Erlich unlawfully posted to the newsgroup works from two separate categories of writings by Hubbard which are contained in Exhibits A and B of the FAC. Following Hubbard's death in 1986, ownership of Hubbard's copyrights passed to Author's Family Trust-B. In 1993, the copyrights were distributed to the Church of Spiritual Technology ("CST"), a California nonprofit religious corporation.

Plaintiff Bridge Publications, Inc. ("BPI"), a nonprofit branch of the Church, claims to be the exclusive licensee of CST's copyrighted literary works listed in Exhibit A to the Complaint ("Exhibit A works"), which consist mainly of policy letters and bulletins from the Church.

Plaintiff Religious Technology Center ("RTC"), a nonprofit religious corporation, "was formed by Scientologists, with the approval of [Hubbard], to act as the protector of the religion of Scientology and to own, protect, and control the utilization of the Advanced Technology[7] in the United States." FAC, Ex. C, at 2. RTC claims to be the exclusive licensee of the copyrights and the owner of the other rights in the unpublished Advanced Technology works listed in Exhibit B to the Complaint (the "Advanced Technology" works or the "Exhibit B works").

BPI and RTC allege that Erlich infringed the copyrights in the Exhibit A and B works. RTC also alleges that Erlich misappropriated its trade secrets in the Exhibit B works, the confidentiality of which it alleges has been the subject of elaborate security measures. RTC further claims that those works are extremely valuable to the Church. Erlich admits to having posted excerpts from some of the works, but argues that the quotations were used to provide context for debate and as a basis for his criticism.

Erlich further argues that he has neither claimed authorship of any of the works nor personally profited from his critique, satire, and commentary. Erlich contends that all of the Exhibit B documents he posted had been previously Page 1240 posted anonymously over the Internet, except for item 1, which he claims he received anonymously through the mail.

From August to December 1994, plaintiffs exchanged a series of letters with Erlich, warning him to stop posting their protected writings onto the newsgroup. Plaintiffs also demanded that defendants Netcom and Klemesrud take actions to prevent Erlich's continued postings of protected materials. Erlich indicated that he would not stop, claiming he had a right to continue with his criticism and satire. On February 8, 1995, plaintiffs filed this action against Erlich, Klemesrud, and Netcom for copyright infringement and, against Erlich alone, for misappropriation of trade secrets, seeking actual, statutory, and punitive damages, injunctive relief, impoundment of the infringing materials and equipment, and attorneys' fees and costs.

On February 10, 1995, the court granted plaintiffs' ex parte application for a temporary restraining order ("TRO") prohibiting Erlich from making unauthorized use of works identified in the exhibits to the complaint and an order directing the clerk to issue a writ of seizure under 17 U.S.C. § 503(a). On February 13, 1995, in execution of the writ of seizure, local police officers entered Erlich's home to conduct the seizure. The officers were accompanied by several RTC representatives, who aided in the search and seizure of documents related to Erlich's alleged copyright infringement and misappropriation of trade secrets. Erlich alleges that RTC officials in fact directed the seizure, which took approximately seven hours. Erlich alleges that plaintiffs seized books, working papers, and personal papers. After locating Erlich's computers, plaintiffs allegedly seized computer disks and copied portions of Erlich's hard disk drive onto floppy disks and then erased the originals from the hard drive. Although plaintiffs returned to Erlich's counsel some of the articles seized, Erlich contends that plaintiffs have not returned all of the seized articles, including ones that are unrelated to the litigation.

On February 23, 1995, the court issued an "Amended TRO," which sought to clarify what types of use were prohibited and to emphasize that Erlich could make "fair use" of the Exhibit A works.

II. PRELIMINARY INJUNCTION/DISSOLUTION OF TEMPORARY RESTRAINING ORDER[8]

A. Legal Standards

A party seeking a preliminary injunction may establish its entitlement to equitable relief by showing either (1) a combination of probable success on the merits and the possibility of irreparable injury, or (2) serious questions as to these matters and that the balance of hardships tips sharply in its favor. *First Brands Corp. v. Fred Meyer, Inc.*, 809 F.2d 1378, 1381 (9th Cir.1987). These two tests are not separate, but represent a continuum of equitable discretion whereby the greater the relative hardship to the moving party, the less probability of success need be shown. *Regents of University of California v. American Broadcasting Cos.,* 747 F.2d 511, 515 (9th Cir.1984). The primary purpose of a preliminary injunction is to preserve the status quo pending a trial on the merits. *Los Angeles Memorial Coliseum Commission v. National Football League,* 634 F.2d 1197, 1200 (9th Cir.1980).

B. Likelihood of Success on Copyright Infringement Claims

To establish copyright infringement, plaintiffs must demonstrate (1) they own a valid copyright and (2) Erlich violated any of their exclusive rights, including, *inter alia,* the rights to reproduce or prepare derivative works from the original, or to distribute or display copies publicly. 17 U.S.C. §§ 106(1)-(3) & (5), 501(a); *Feist Publications, Inc. v. Rural Telephone Service Co.,* 499 U.S. 340, 361-63, 111 S.Ct. 1282, 1296, 113 L.Ed.2d 358 (1991). Erlich, for the most part, admits to having "copied" the Exhibit A and B works, but contends that plaintiffs are not able to

Page 1241

establish ownership of a valid copyright interest in those works. Erlich also argues that his activities do not constitute infringement because his use was a "fair use."

1. Ownership of a Valid Copyright

Proof of ownership of an existing, valid, and registered copyright interest is a statutory prerequisite to filing an infringement action. 17 U.S.C. § 411. Registration, when "made before or within five years after first publication of the work[,] shall constitute prima facie evidence of the validity of the copyright," including originality, compliance with statutory formalities, and copyrightability. *Id.,* § 410(c); 3 Melville B. Nimmer & David Nimmer, *Nimmer on Copyright* (1995) ("Nimmer") § 12.11[B]. When registration is made more than five years after first publication, the evidentiary weight of the certificate of registration is within the court's discretion. *Id.* § 12.11[A], [B]. When the plaintiff is not the author of a work, he must provide evidence of a chain of title from the registrant to him. Nimmer § 12.11[C].

Plaintiffs provide evidence of registration for all of the Exhibit A and B works. *See* FAC, Ex. H. Plaintiffs further provide copies of assignment and licensing agreements purportedly showing the necessary chain of title from Hubbard, the author of the works, to plaintiffs RTC and BPI. Attached to the FAC are assignments of all rights in the Advanced Technology works from Hubbard and his estate to RTC. *Id.*, Exs. C, D, F & G. Under the "Literary Agreement" attached to the FAC, BPI is the exclusive licensee of various published, non-fiction Hubbard works, including those works in Exhibit A to the FAC. *Id.*, Ex. E.

Erlich sets forth in his "Appendix re: Copyright Issues" a host of purported irregularities and defects with the registrations, maintaining that plaintiffs have failed to prove a likelihood of success on ownership of many, if not all, of the works. The court finds that, except as to item 4 of Exhibit A, Erlich has failed to rebut the presumption of validity.

Erlich's contention that item 4 of Exhibit A ("20 Nov 1961, Routine 3D Commands") has fallen into the public domain appears to be correct. The registration for item 4 gives a first publication date of 1961. Under the Copyright Act of 1909 ("the 1909 Act"), which still applies to works that were first published prior to January 1, 1964, an author is entitled to an initial 28-year copyright term, which expires unless the copyright is renewed by the author or his statutory successors during the final year of the initial term. 2 Nimmer § 9.05[B][1]. The copyright notice date on item 4 is evidence that the work was first published in 1961. *See New Era Publications International, ApS v. Carol Publishing Group,* 729 F.Supp. 992, 995 (S.D.N.Y.), *aff'd in part, rev'd in part,*https://apps.fastcase.com

/Research/Pages/Document.aspx?LTID=v%2

b%2bWn0pFJOPw

Vn7bDpURwR5rY%2bXX9Uta8hAwg5stZDj8sEobQk

SQ%2bky

70Tw1SszD6GuoylZ859kfbr0CHnkdXRmwxLW7cJtCJ

ym88G

mTgsrrExWnNNSNiN61CAkvo365&ECF=904+F.2d+1

52 904 F.2d 152

(2d Cir.), *cert. denied,*https://apps.fastcase.com/Research/Pages/Document.aspx?LTID=v%2b%2bWn0pFJOPwVn7bDpUR wR5rY%2bXX9Uta8hAwg5stZDj8sEobQkSQ%2bky70Tw1S szD6GuoylZ859kfbr0CHnkdXRmwxLW7cJtCJym88GmTgsrrEx WnNNSNiN61CAkvo365&ECF=498+U.S.+921 498 U.S. 921,

111 S.Ct. 297, 112 L.Ed.2d 251 (1990). Because there is no evidence that the copyright for item 4 was renewed in 1989, 28 years after its initial publication, the court finds that it fell into the public domain and cannot be the subject of an action for infringement. *See id.* Plaintiffs argue, however, that item 4 was part of a collection that was registered in 1976, the year that it was first published. As such, plaintiffs contend that the collective work is not yet subject to renewal. While those parts of the 1976 collection that were first published in 1976 were not subject to renewal in 1989, those previously published portions of the collection, such as item 4, must still be timely renewed

notwithstanding the registration as a collection in 1976. *See* 1 Nimmer §§ 3.07[C], 3.04[A], at 3-19.

Erlich's next claim is that plaintiffs have not registered the works that were infringed, but only the compilations in which they were included.

Where, as here, the author of a collection or derivative work is also the author of the preexisting work, registration of the collection is sufficient. *Abend v. MCA, Inc.,* 863 F.2d 1465, 1471-72 (9th Cir.1988), *aff'd,*https://apps.fastcase.com/Research/Pages/Document.aspx?LTID=v%2b%2bWn0pFJOPwVn7bDpURwR5rY%2bXX9Uta8hAwg5stZDj8sEobQkSQ%2bky70Tw1SszD6GuoylZ859kfbr0CHnkdXRmwxLW7cJtCJym88GmTgsrrExWnNNSNiN61CAkvo365&ECF=495+U.S.+207 495 U.S. 207, 110

S.Ct. 1750, 109 L.Ed.2d 184 (1990); 2 Nimmer § 7.16[B][2], at 7-

168 to -170 (distinguishing this situation from that where copyright owner of collective work is not also

the owner of the preexisting work). Here, Hubbard was the author of the underlying work and was also the author of the collection of his own works. Accordingly, registration of the collections Page 1242 that include the Exhibit A works constitutes registration of the underlying works.

Erlich's next argument, that plaintiffs have not shown that Hubbard's statutory successors assigned the renewal terms of the copyrights to plaintiffs, is clearly rebutted by the evidence. *See* Hawkins Decl., Exs. A-I. The Exhibit B works do not require renewal because they were unpublished as of January 1, 1978, the effective date of the Copyright Act of 1976 ("the 1976 Act"), and were thus protected only by common law copyright. *See* 2 Nimmer § 9.01[B][2], at 9-17 to -18. As of January 1, 1978, these works became protected by statutory copyright under the new scheme of the 1976 Act, which does not require renewal. *Id.*

Finally, Erlich contends that the automatic statutory presumption of validity does not apply because many of the works were published more than five years before registration. The dates specified in a copyright notice are evidence of the date of publication. *New Era,*https://apps.fastcase.com/Research/Pages/Document.aspx?LTID=v%2b%2bWn0pFJOPwVn7bDpURwR5rY%2bXX9Uta8hAwg 5stZDj8sEobQkSQ%2bky70Tw1SszD6GuoylZ859kfbr0CHnkdXRmwxLW7cJtCJym88GmTgsrrExWnNNSNiN61CAkvo365&ECF=729+F.Supp.+at+995 729 F.Supp. at 995. As to the unpublished[9] Exhibit B works, registrations were made before first publication in accordance with section 410(c) and thus the presumption is still valid. However, it appears Erlich is correct that the statutory presumption does not apply as to items 1, 2, 4, 5, 6, 7, and 8 of Exhibit A. It is within the court's discretion what weight to give the copyright registrations in determining the validity of the copyright interests of those works for which plaintiffs are not entitled to an automatic presumption of validity. In light of plaintiffs' evidence of validity, *see* Hawkins Decl., and the lack of a persuasive challenge to the validity of the copyrights by Erlich, the court finds that plaintiffs' registrations are strong evidence of the validity of their claimed copyrights.[10]

2. Direct Infringement

Except as to item 9 of Exhibit A and item 9 of Exhibit B, *see* Oakley May 12, 1995 Decl., Ex. B, Erlich does not dispute that he engaged in "copying," which would constitute direct infringement under section 106. As to the item 9 works, there is no evidence that Erlich ever made any postings of or otherwise copied those items. The court will therefore consider plaintiffs' infringement claims as to the remaining works.[11]

3. Fair Use Defense

"Infringement" consists of violating the author's exclusive rights. 17

U.S.C. § 501. Although the author has the exclusive rights to reproduce, distribute, and display a copyrighted work under section 106, these rights are limited by the defense[12] of "fair use":

Notwithstanding the provisions of section 106 and 106A, the fair use of a copyrighted work, including such use by reproduction

Page 1243

in copies ... or by any other means specified in that section, for purposes such as criticism, comment, news reporting, teaching (including multiple copies for classroom use), scholarship, or research, is not an infringement of copyright.

17 U.S.C. § 107 (emphasis added). The defense "permits and requires courts to avoid rigid application of the copyright statute when, on occasion, it would stifle the very creativity which that law is designed to foster." *Campbell v. Acuff-Rose Music, Inc.*, 510 U.S. 569, , 114 S.Ct. 1164, 1170, 127 L.Ed.2d 500 (1994) (citation omitted). Congress has set out four nonexclusive factors to be considered in determining the availability of the fair use defense:

1. The purpose and character of the use, including whether such use is of a commercial nature or is for nonprofit educational purposes;
2. The nature of the copyrighted work;
3. The amount and substantiality of the portion used in relation to the copyrighted work as a whole; and

4. The effect of the use upon the potential market for or value of the copyrighted work.

17 U.S.C. § 107. The fair use doctrine calls for a case-by-case analysis. *Campbell,*https://apps.fastcase.com/Research/Pages/Document.aspx?LTID=v%2b%2bWn0pFJOPwVn7bDpURwR5r Y%2bXX9Uta8hAwg5stZDj8sEobQkSQ%2bky70Tw1SszD6Guo ylZ859kfbr0CHnkdXRmwxLW7cJtCJym 88GmTgsrrExWnNNSN iN61CAkvo365&ECF=510+U.S.+at+ 510 U.S. at , 114

S.Ct. at 1170. All of the factors "are to be explored, and the results weighed together, in light of the purposes of copyright." *Id.*https://apps.fastcase.com/Research/Pages/Document.aspx?LTID=v%2b%2bWn0pFJOPwVn7bDpURwR5r Y%2bXX9Uta8hAwg5s tZDj8sEobQkSQ%2bky70Tw1SszD6GuoylZ859kfbr0C HnkdXR mwxLW7cJtCJym88Gm TgsrrExWnNNSNiN61CAkvo365&EC F=510+U.S.+at+510 U.S. at - , 114 S.Ct. at 1170-71.

First Factor: Purpose and Character of the Use

The first statutory factor looks to the purpose and character of the defendant's use. Erlich argues that his use was criticism, which is one of those uses listed in the preamble to section 107. Similarly, Erlich maintains that his use was meant to "evoke discussion regarding various Scientology philosophies." Mot. To Dissolve at

22. Use for the purpose of criticism weighs in favor of fair use. *See New Era,*https://apps.fastcase.com/Research/Pages/Document.aspx ?LTID=v%2b %2bWn0pFJOPwVn7bDpURwR5rY%2bXX9Uta 8hAwg5stZDj8sEobQkS Q%2bky70Tw1SszD6GuoylZ859kfbr0C HnkdXRmwxLW7cJtCJym88Gm TgsrrExWnNNSNiN61CAkvo 365&ECF=904+F.2d+at+156-57 904 F.2d at 156-57 (using

Hubbard's works in critical biography meets first factor for fair use). Plaintiffs contest Erlich's characterizations of his use, claiming that most of Erlich's postings were verbatim copies, with little or no added comment or criticism.[13] Plaintiffs further contend that Erlich's purpose was spite or some other destructive reason. However, plaintiffs give no explanation as to why Erlich's purpose was other than to criticize or to evoke discussion regarding Scientology. Because there is insufficient evidence to support plaintiffs' claim that Erlich's copying was made out of spite or for other destructive reasons, the court will assume Erlich's intended purpose was criticism or comment.

Transformative Use

Plaintiffs' argument that the amount of added criticism belies Erlich's critical purpose can also be construed as an attack on the "transformative" nature of Erlich's use. In *Campbell,* the Supreme Court held that the central purpose of the first inquiry is to determine whether the new work is transformative (also described as "productive"), that is, whether it "adds something new, with a further purpose or different character, altering the first with new expression, meaning, or message." 510 U.S. at , 114 S.Ct. at 1171. Erlich's use is only minimally transformative since, unlike the typical critic, Erlich adds little new expression to the Church's works.

Accordingly, despite Erlich's purported critical purpose, the actual character of his use does not weigh heavily in his favor because it has only a slight transformative nature. In any case, the Supreme Court held in *Sony Corp. of America v. Universal City Studios, Inc.,* 464 U.S. 417, 455 n. 40, 104 S.Ct. 774, 795 n. 40, 78 L.Ed.2d 574

(1984) that the fair use defense is not "rigidly circumscribed" by the productive use requirement. The Court found that a home viewer's verbatim copying of copyrighted television shows for the purposes of time shifting was fair use even though there was only a minimal showing of increased convenience to the home user.

Page 1244

Commercial Nature of Use

Where the use is not highly transformative, as here, the court will focus on whether the use is of a commercial nature. The *Campbell* Court emphasized that a commercial use does not dictate against a finding of fair use, as most of the uses listed in the statute are "generally conducted for profit in this country." 510 U.S. at , 114 S.Ct. at 1174. Nonetheless, the Court recognized that a commercial use weighs against a finding of fair use. *Id.* The fact that there is no evidence that Erlich gains financially from his criticism of the Church weighs in his favor.

Plaintiffs argue, however, that Erlich personally gains through increased status and recognition among his peers and the public. In *Weissmann v. Freeman*, 868 F.2d 1313 (2d Cir.), *cert.*

*denied,*https://apps.fastcase.com/Research/Pages/Document.aspx? LTID=v %2b%2bWn0pFJOPwVn7bDpURwR5rY%2bXX9Uta8 hAwg5stZ Dj8sEob QkSQ%2bky70Tw1SszD6GuoylZ859kfbr0CHnkdXRm wxLW7cJt CJym88 GmTgsrrExWnNNSNiN61CAkvo365&ECF=493+U.S.+883 493 U.S. 883,

110 S.Ct. 219, 107 L.Ed.2d 172 (1989), the Second Circuit recognized that, in the unusual setting of academia, a defendant can profit personally from copying despite the lack of a monetary gain. The defendant in *Weissmann* was a professor who copied a former assistant's scholarly work, used it for the same

purpose as the author, and claimed credit for himself, thereby aiding his professional advancement. *Id.* at 1324. Here, there is neither evidence that Erlich took credit for any of plaintiffs' works nor that he is personally profiting, professionally or otherwise, as a result of his postings. If mere recognition by one's peers constituted "personal profit" to defeat a finding of a noncommercial use, courts would seldom find any criticism fair use and much valuable criticism would be discouraged. Thus, the court finds that *Weissmann* is inapplicable here, and that its holding should not be stretched to swallow all nonprofit criticism motivated by concern for status. Accordingly, based on the clearly noncommercial nature of the use and the protected purpose of criticism, the court finds that the first fair use factor weighs slightly in Erlich's favor despite the minimally transformative nature of Erlich's use.

Defendant's Conduct

Plaintiffs contend that, regardless of the results of weighing the four fair use factors, a finding of fair use is nonetheless precluded because Erlich's copies were made not from legitimate copies of the works but from unauthorized copies. Although plaintiffs discuss this purported "good faith" prerequisite[14] to fair use apart from the four factors, it is properly a factor to be considered with the first statutory factor regarding the character of the use. 3 Nimmer § 13.05[A][1][d], at 13-171 to -174 (discussing "defendant's conduct" as one aspect of the first statutory factor).

The court finds that plaintiffs' showing on bad faith is mixed at best.

There is no evidence here that Erlich obtained his copies of plaintiffs' works through deceit. *Cf.*

*Atari,*https://apps.fastcase.com/Research/Pages/Document.aspx?L TID=v%2b%2bWn0pFJOPwVn7bDpURwR5rY%2bXX9Uta8hA wg5stZDj8sEobQ kSQ%2bky70Tw1SszD6GuoylZ859kfbr0CHn kdXRmwxLW7cJtCJym88G mTgsrrExWnNNSNiN61CAkvo365 &ECF=975+F.2d+at+836%2c+843 975 F.2d at 836, 843 (finding no fair use where defendant obtained plaintiff's source code by lying to copyright office).

Page 1245

Unlike *Sega,* there is no admission by the defendant that he does not possess *any* legal copies. As to several of the Exhibit A works, it appears that Erlich possessed legitimate, published books containing some of the works; plaintiffs offer no evidence that Erlich obtained these books in some unlawful or illegitimate manner.[15] However, as to those works where Erlich claims he obtained his copies over the Internet or anonymously through the mail, this does not negate an inference that he received those copies in an improper manner. Erlich's copies of Exhibit B works were more likely unauthorized than not; plaintiffs have provided substantial evidence that the Advanced Technology works are kept confidential, *see infra* part II.C.2, and that Erlich would not have been given permission to keep a copy of those works. For most of the disputed works, the fact that Erlich may have obtained his copies in an unauthorized manner tends to weigh in plaintiffs' favor. This finding, however, will not bar Erlich's fair use defense, but will merely be considered with the other factors.

Second Factor: Nature of the Copyrighted Work

The second factor focuses on two different aspects of the copyrighted work: whether it is published or unpublished and whether it is informational or creative.

Published vs. Unpublished

The unpublished status of a work is "a critical element of its nature.'"

*Harper & Row,*https://apps.fastcase.com/Research/Pages/Docume nt.aspx?LTID=v%2 b%2bWn0pFJOPwVn7bDpURwR5rY%2bXX 9Uta8hAwg5stZDj8sEobQk SQ%2bky70Tw1SszD6GuoylZ859kf br0CHnkdXRmwxLW7cJtCJym88G mTgsrrExWnNNSNiN61CA kvo365&ECF=471+U.S.+at+564 471 U.S. at 564, 105 S.Ct. at 2232 (finding no fair use where *The Nation* magazine used unpublished manuscript to scoop *Time* magazine). The *Nation* case held that "the scope of fair use is narrower with respect to unpublished works." *Id.* In a case involving copying of allegedly unpublished works by Hubbard, the Second Circuit recognized that where the works were unpublished no court had yet found in favor of the infringer on the second factor.

New Era

https://apps.fastcase.com/Research/Pages/Document.aspx?LTI D=v%2b%2bWn0pFJOPwVn7bDpURwR5rY%2bXX9 Uta8hAwg 5stZDj8sEobQkSQ%2bky70Tw1SszD6GuoylZ859kfbr 0CHnkdX RmwxLW7cJtCJym88GmTgsrrExWnNNSNiN61CAkv o365&EC F=904+F.2d+at+155 904 F.2d at 155. Nevertheless, the Second Circuit affirmed a finding of fair use where a biographer quoted portions of unpublished letters. *Wright v. Warner Books, Inc.,* 953 F.2d 731 (2d Cir.1991); *see also* *Norse v. Henry Holt & Co.,* 847 F.Supp. 142, 147 (N.D.Cal.1994) (finding fair use where 50 words copied from unpublished letters and all but the second factor weighed in favor of defendant). In 1992, Congress amended section 107 of the 1976 Act to clarify that the unpublished nature of a work should not itself bar a finding of fair use. *See* H.R.Rep. No. 102-286, 102d Cong., 2d Sess. 8 (1992) (House Report) (citing *Wright* with approval and criticizing earlier Second Circuit decisions that created a per se rule against fair use of unpublished works); *see also* 3 Nimmer § 13.05[A][2], at 13-184 to -186. Congress construed the *Nation*'s statement that the *scope* of fair use is narrower for unpublished works to mean that the *amount* of permissible copying will be less in the case of an unpublished work. *Id.*

Even though a work is read by a large group of people, it is still unpublished where it is held confidential and the authors do not relinquish control over their copies of the work. *See College Entrance Examination Board v. Cuomo*, 788 F.Supp. 134, 139-41 (N.D.N.Y.1992) (finding that administered secure tests were necessarily unpublished because author did not relinquish control and finding for author on second fair use factor).

Plaintiffs have adequately demonstrated that the Exhibit B Advanced Technology works are kept confidential using tight security measures. *See infra* part II.C.3. Although there is evidence that individuals may have made unauthorized public disclosures of some of these works, *see id.*, the works are still "unpublished" for the purposes of the fair use defense. *See* discussion *supra* note 9. However, the Exhibit A works, with one exception, are published. Accordingly, this portion of the second factor weighs in Erlich's

Page 1246

favor as to the published Exhibit A works and strongly in plaintiffs' favor as to the Exhibit B works.

Informational vs. Creative

The second aspect of this factor looks to broaden the protection of those works that are creative, fictional, or highly original and lessen the protection for those works that are factual, informational, or functional. *See Campbell,*

https://apps.fastcase.com/Research/Pages

/Document.aspx?LTID=v%2b%2bWn0pFJOPwVn7bD

pURwR5r

Y%2bXX9Uta8hAwg5stZDj8sEobQkSQ%2bky70Tw1S

szD6Guo

ylZ859kfbr0CHnkdXRmwxLW7cJtCJym88GmTgsrrEx

WnNNSN iN61CAkvo365&ECF=510+U.S.+at+_510

U.S. at , 114

S.Ct. at 1175. The Second Circuit noted the obvious difficulty in applying this test in a case involving a large number of works by Hubbard:

We agree ... that there is no easy distinction between works that are "factual" on the one hand, and "creative" or "expressive" on the other, because "`[c]reation of a nonfiction work, even a compilation of pure fact, entails originality.'" Thus, reasonable people can disagree over how to classify Hubbard's works.

*New Era,*https://apps.fastcase.com/Research/Pages/Document.aspx?LTID=v%2b%2bWn0pFJOPwVn7bDpURwR5rY%2bXX9Uta8hAwg5stZDj8sEobQkSQ%2bky70Tw1SszD6GuoylZ859kfbr0CHnkdXRmwxLW7cJtCJym88GmTgsrrExWnNNSNiN61CAkvo365&EC F=904+F.2d+at+158 904 F.2d at 158 (citations omitted). The Second Circuit concluded that "although some of the quoted passages can accurately be described as expressive — e.g., Hubbard's poetry — our review of the record persuades us that most simply cannot be so characterized." A district judge in this Circuit, considering works that are part of the Church's Advanced Technology, concluded that "Hubbard's works are the product of his creative thought process, and not merely informational."[16] *Bridge Publications, Inc. v. Vien,* 827 F.Supp. 629, 635-36 (S.D.Cal.1993).

In the present case, this court also finds the task of categorizing Hubbard's writings difficult. In their complaint, plaintiffs describe Hubbard as the author of "original works on applied religious philosophy and spiritual healing technology, including training materials and course manuals of the Scientology religion." FAC ¶ 9. In reviewing the Exhibit A works, which are predominantly "policy letters" of the Hubbard Communications Office, the court finds that these works, although creative, are primarily functional or instructive. Item 1 of Exhibit B, the Class VIII "Assists" Tape, appears more original and creative than the other works, and is thus deserving of greater fair use protection. The remaining Exhibit B works, however, are part of the methodology of the Church's "applied religious philosophy," and as such are more instructive and functional than fictional. This court is not convinced, however, that this factor should play a major role in the context of religious works, which do not easily fit into the creative/informational dichotomy.

Because the Exhibit B works are unpublished and large portions of them were copied by Erlich, *see infra* part II.B.3.c, this factor weighs heavily against Erlich with respect to those works, despite the informational nature of most of them. The Exhibit A works, however, are published and primarily informational, and this factor weighs in favor of Erlich as to those works.

Third Factor: Amount and Substantiality of the Portion Used

The third factor concerns both the percentage of the original work that was copied, and whether that portion constitutes the "heart" of the copyrighted work. *Harper & Row,*https://apps.fastcase.com/Research/Pages/Document.aspx?LTID=v%2b%2bWn0pFJOPwVn7bDpURwR5rY%2bXX9Uta8hAwg5stZDj8sEobQkSQ%2bky70T w1SszD6GuoylZ859kfbr0CHnkdXRmwxLW7cJtCJym 88GmTgsr rExWnNNSNiN61CAkvo365&ECF=471+U.S.+at+564-65 471

U.S. at 564-65, 105 S.Ct. at 2232-33. The copying of an entire work will ordinarily militate against a finding of fair use, although this is not a per se rule.

*Sony,*https://apps.fastcase.com/Research/Pages/Document.aspx?LT ID=v%2b%2bWn0pFJOPwVn7bDpURwR5rY%2bXX9 Uta8hAw g5stZDj8sEobQkSQ%2bky70Tw1SszD6GuoylZ859kfb r0CHnkdX RmwxLW7cJtCJym88GmTgsrrExWnNNSNiN61CAkv o365&EC F=464+U.S.+at+449-450 464 U.S. at 449-450, 104 S.Ct. at 792 (finding exception to this rule for time-shifting by home viewers to enable them to see works that they were invited to see in their *entirety* free of charge). The amount of copying that is acceptable will depend on the character of the use and degree to which the copy transforms the original.

*Campbell,*https://apps.fastcase.com/Research/Pages /Document.asp x?LTID=v%2b%2bWn0pFJOPwVn7bDpURwR5rY%2b XX9Uta8 hAwg5stZDj8sEobQkSQ%2bky70Tw1SszD6GuoylZ85 9kfbr0CH nkdXRmwxLW7cJtCJym88GmTgsrrExWnNNSNiN61 CAkvo365 &ECF=510+U.S.+at+510 U.S. at, 114 S.Ct. at 1175-76 (finding parody can copy enough of original to "conjure [it] up" so the audience will recognize what is being parodied). Less copying will be acceptable where the original is unpublished. *See* 3 Nimmer § 13.05[A][2], at 13-185 n. 200.

Plaintiffs allege that Erlich's postings copy substantial amounts of the originals or, in some cases, the entire works.

Page 1247

Erlich responds that, as to some of the copied works, the original documents are actually only a small part of a larger collection. *See* Oakley Reply Decl., Ex. C. Erlich claims that the court should look at the entire registered collective work to determine the percentage of that work which Erlich copied. However, the Ninth Circuit held in *Hustler Magazine, Inc. v. Moral Majority, Inc.*, 796 F.2d 1148, 1155 (9th

Cir.1986) that "[a] creative work does not deserve less protection just because it is part of composite work." The Second Circuit held in *American Geophysical Union v. Texaco, Inc.*, 802 F.Supp. 1, 17 (S.D.N.Y.1992),

*aff'd,*https://apps.fastcase.com/Research/Pages/Document.aspx?LT ID=v%2b%2bWn0pFJOPwVn7bDpURwR5rY%2bXX9 Uta8hAw g5stZDj8sEobQkSQ%2bky70Tw1SszD6GuoylZ859kfb r0CHnkdX RmwxLW7cJtCJym88GmTgsrrExWnNNSNiN61CAkv o365&EC F=37+F.3d+881+%282d+Cir.1994%29 37 F.3d 881 (2d Cir.1994) that copying an entire article from a journal whose copyright has been registered as a whole still constitutes copying the entire work. Similarly, here, although many of Hubbard's lectures, policy statements, and course packets are collected into larger volumes, and registered as a whole, they may still constitute separate works for the purposes of this factor.

It appears Erlich copied all or almost all of many of the works,[17] which were predominantly short documents of less than three pages, and mostly with no comments or with very brief comments[18] at the beginning or end.

See McShane February 27, 1995 Decl., Ex. A, B, C-1. The court further finds that where Erlich only copied a portion of a work, that portion constituted the "heart" of the work. *Compare* February 27, 1995 App. in Support of Warren McShane, Exs. 1A-188A *with* 1B- 188B; *see* *Harper & Row,*https://apps.fastcase.com/Research

/Pages/Document.aspx?LTID=v%2b%2bWn0pFJO PwVn7bDpUR wR5rY%2bXX9Uta8hAwg5stZDj8sEobQkSQ%2bky70 Tw1SszD 6GuoylZ859kfbr0CHnkdXRmwxLW7cJtCJym88GmT gsrrExWnN NSNiN61CAkvo365&ECF=471+U.S.+at+564-65 471 U.S. at 564-

65, 105 S.Ct. at 2232-33 (finding quotation of 300 out of 200,000 words that were "essentially the heart of the book" not fair use).

Accordingly, this factor weighs heavily in plaintiffs' favor, especially as to the unpublished works, where the amount of acceptable copying is even lower.

Page 1248

Fourth Factor: Effect of the Use upon the Potential Market for the Work

The fourth and final statutory factor concerns "the extent of market harm caused by the particular actions of the alleged infringer" and "`whether unrestricted and widespread conduct of the sort engaged in by the defendant ... would result in a substantially adverse impact on the potential market' for the original."

*Campbell,*https://apps.fastcase.com/Research/Pages/Document.asp
x?LTID=v%2b%2bWn0pFJOPwVn7bDpURwR5rY%2b
XX9Uta8
hAwg5stZDj8sEobQkSQ%2bky70Tw1SszD6GuoylZ85
9kfbr0CH
nkdXRmwxLW7cJtCJym88GmTgsrrExWnNNSNiN61
CAkvo365 &ECF=510+U.S.+at+ 510 U.S. at _, 114 S.Ct. at 1177 (quoting 3 Nimmer § 13.05[A][4]) (remanding for consideration of this factor). Although the results of all four factors must be weighed together, *id.* at_,

114 S.Ct. at 1171, the fourth factor is central to the fair use analysis, 3 Nimmer § 13.05[A][4], at 13-188 to -189 (citing *Harper &*

*Row,*https://apps.fastcase.com/Research/Pages/Document.aspx?LT ID=v%2b%2bWn0pFJOPwVn7bDpURwR5rY%2bXX9 Uta8hAw g5stZDj8sEobQkSQ%2bky70Tw1SszD6GuoylZ859kfb r0CHnkdX RmwxLW7cJtCJym88GmTgsrrExWnNNSNiN61CAkv o365&EC F=471+U.S.+at+566 471 U.S. at 566, 105 S.Ct. at 2233), 13-207 (observing that fourth factor explains results in recent Supreme Court cases).

Plaintiffs contend that Erlich's posting of plaintiffs' copyrighted works over the Internet, where more than 25 million subscribers could access them, could potentially have a detrimental effect on plaintiffs. Plaintiffs point to the fact that, in the past, the Church has faced "ex-parishioners using copyrighted materials to set up and market `religious' training adapted from the Scientology religion." Pltfs.' Opp'n at 39. In *Vien,* the defendant had left the Church of Scientology to start her own competing ministry, taking with her some of the Church's Advanced Technology works, which she used in her courses and offered for sale. 827 F.Supp. at 632-34. The court held that "since defendant uses the works for the same purpose intended by plaintiffs, it appears defendant's unauthorized copies fulfill the `demand for the original' works and `diminish or prejudice' their potential sale." *Id.* at 636.

Plaintiffs' case is not as strong here as it was in *Vien.* The demand of those seeking out the Church's religious training will hardly be met by Erlich's postings.[19] Even if Erlich's copying of plaintiffs' works were not for a critical purpose, plaintiffs would still have not shown that Erlich's postings diminish the demand by Church followers in the courses.

According to the Church, these courses must be studied in a systematic fashion, following one "course" at a time, with proper guidance. McShane May 31, 1995 Decl. 7-8; *see Wollersheim,*https://apps.fastcase.com/Research/Pages/Document.a
spx?LTID=v%2b%2bWn0pFJOPwVn7bDpURwR5rY%2bXX9Ut

a8hAwg5stZDj8sEobQkSQ%2bky70Tw1SszD6GuoylZ
859kfbr0C
HnkdXRmwxLW7cJtCJym88GmTgsrrExWnNNSNiN
61CAkvo36 5&ECF=796+F.2d+at+1091 796 2d at 1091
(noting RTC's argument that Advanced Technology works are trade secrets whose misappropriation would cause "`religious harm' ... [to] adherents from premature unsupervised exposure to the materials").

Although many of Erlich's postings contain much of an original work, each of these works is only a small portion of the teachings necessary for a particular "course." *See* Oakley Reply Decl., Ex. C. For the most part, Erlich's postings are sporadic and incomplete. The court is thus not convinced that postings like Erlich's could be effectively used by rival Scientology-like religious groups. Moreover, there is no evidence that the Church currently faces any competition by ex-parishioners, *see* Oakley Reply Decl., Ex. B., McShane Depo. at 95, although there is circumstantial evidence that such competition could occur in the future, based on the fact that several groups have competed with the Church in the past. *See id.* at 93-94.

There is little evidence of a systematic attempt by Erlich at posting the complete works necessary for setting up a competing religious group. It seems unlikely, although possible, that Erlich's postings, if continued and expanded, could supply such a group with the means to compete with plaintiffs. *See* discussion *infra* part II.B.3. While the demand for a particular work may be suppressed through criticism, it is unlikely that the demand for the Church's unique ability to provide parishioners with a complete and guided access to the various course materials will be suppressed. The court finds it unlikely that Erlich's noncommercial use, or widespread conduct like Erlich's use by others, would diminish or prejudice the potential sale of plaintiffs' works, interfere with their

Page 1249

marketability, or fulfill the demand for the works. *See Maxtone- Graham v. Burtchaell,* 803 F.2d 1253, 1264 (2d Cir.1986), *cert.*

*denied,*https://apps.fastcase.com/Research/Pages/Document.aspx?LTID=v%2b%2bWn0pFJOPwVn7bDpURwR5rY%2bX

X9Uta8h
Awg5stZDj8sEobQkSQ%2bky70Tw1SszD6GuoylZ859
kfbr0CHn
kdXRmwxLW7cJtCJym88GmTgsrrExWnNNSNiN61C
Akvo365& ECF=481+U.S.+1059 481 U.S. 1059, 107 S.Ct. 2201, 95 L.Ed.2d

856 (1987) (finding no market harm where pro-choice work was excerpted in antiabortion book because of differing viewpoints and editorial formats);

*Hustler,*https://apps.fastcase.com/Research/Pages/Document.aspx?
LTID=v%2b%2bWn0pFJOPwVn7bDpURwR5rY%2bX
X9Uta8h
Awg5stZDj8sEobQkSQ%2bky70Tw1SszD6GuoylZ859
kfbr0CHn
kdXRmwxLW7cJtCJym88GmTgsrrExWnNNSNiN61C
Akvo365& ECF=796+F.2d+at+1155-56 796 F.2d at 1155-56;

ReligiousCenter v. Lerma, 897 F.Supp. 260, 265 (E.D.Va.1995) (finding fair use defense probably valid in part because no separate market for Advanced Technology works where Scientologists cannot effectively use them without the Church's supervision);

*Religious Technology Center v. F.A.C.T.NET, Inc.,*https://apps.fast case.com/Research/Pages/Document.aspx?LTID=v%2 b%2bWn0p FJOPwVn7bDpURwR5rY%2bXX9Uta8hAwg5stZDj8s EobQkSQ

%2bky70Tw1SszD6Guoy1Z859kfbr0CHnkdXRmw xLW7cJtCJym 88GmTgsrrExWnNNSNiN61CAkvo365&ECF=901+F.S upp.+151

9%2c+1524- 26+%28D.Colo.1995%29 901 F.Supp. 1519, 1524-26 (D.Colo.1995) (finding valid fair use defense because financial harm to the Church was unlikely and there was no showing of a potential effect on the market for plaintiffs' works). Accordingly, the court finds that this factor weighs in Erlich's favor.

Equitable Balancing

In balancing the various factors, the court finds that the percentage of plaintiffs' works copied combined with the minimal added criticism or commentary negates a finding of fair use. Although criticism is a favored use, where that "criticism" consists of copying large portions of plaintiffs' works — and sometimes all of those works — with often no more than one line of criticism, the fair use defense is inappropriate. Erlich has not adequately justified his copying verbatim large portions of plaintiffs' works. The amount of copying was particularly unacceptable with the unpublished Exhibit B works.

While copying all or most of a work does not necessarily preclude fair use, those cases recognizing fair use for complete copying are easily distinguishable. Although the *Sony* Court found acceptable the copying of entire television shows with no added content, this was necessary for the purpose of time-shifting. Unlike Erlich, the time-shifters in *Sony* were already given permission to view the works in their entirety for free. *Sony*,https://apps.fastcase.com/Research/Pages/Document.aspx?LTID=v%2b%2bWn0pFJOPwVn7bDpURwR5rY%2bXX9Uta8hAw g5stZDj8sEobQkSQ%2bky70Tw1SszD6GuoylZ859kfb r0CHnkdX RmwxLW7cJtCJym88GmTgsrrExWnNNSNiN61CAkv o365&EC F=464+U.S.+at+449-450 464 U.S. at 449-450, 104 S.Ct. at 792. The

Court further noted in *Sony* that time-shifters are just as likely to buy prerecorded videos as live viewers, and thus there is no effect on the market for the original. *Id.* at 450 n. 33, 104 S.Ct. at 792 n. 33. The case that perhaps best supports Erlich's position, *Belmore,* is also distinguishable. *See supra* note 17. The original work copied verbatim in *Belmore* was shorter than many of the works Erlich copied and the added criticism in *Belmore* was far longer than most of the criticism that Erlich made. 880 F.Supp. at 678-79. Additionally, unlike the district court in *Belmore,* this court does not find reasonable Erlich's claim that he copied no more than was necessary for his purpose. Moreover, this court is not convinced that *Belmore* is supported by Ninth Circuit law. *See Supermarket of Homes, Inc. v. San Fernando Valley Board of Realtors,* 786 F.2d 1400, 1409 (9th Cir.1986) ("Generally, no more of a work may be taken than is necessary to make the accompanying comment understandable.").

While use of a large percentage or the "heart" of the copyrighted work does not rule out fair use *per se,* other factors are not sufficiently in Erlich's favor to overcome this third factor. Further, the second factor weighs strongly against Erlich as to the unpublished works. The almost verbatim copying here shows that Erlich's work is only minimally transformative and that it is unlikely that Erlich is "truly pursuing a different functional milieu" from the original. 3 Nimmer § 13.05[D][1], at 13-231. In addition, as to the unpublished materials, Erlich's use of possibly illicit copies of those works weighs against him. Thus, Erlich's showing on the first factor is not very strong despite his critical purpose. Similarly, Erlich's showing on the fourth factor does not persuasively suggest fair use.

If Erlich's use were to become widespread, it could potentially have an effect on the market for plaintiffs' works by supplying future splinter groups with the materials needed to compete with the Church. The court views this potentiality as somewhat remote. Nevertheless, given plaintiffs' very strong showing on the third factor, the court finds that, on balance, the equities do not favor a finding of fair use. The case against fair use is even more compelling

Page 1250

for the unpublished works.[20] *But see*

*Lerma,*https://apps.fastcase.com/Research/Pages/Document.aspx?L
TID=v%2b%2bWn0pFJOPwVn7bDpURwR5rY%2bXX
9Uta8hA
wg5stZDj8sEobQkSQ%2bky70Tw1SszD6GuoylZ859kf
br0CHnkd
XRmwxLW7cJtCJym88GmTgsrrExWnNNSNiN61CA
kvo365&E CF=897+F.Supp.+at+265 897 F.Supp. at 265 (order denying temporary restraining order against defendant Washington Post from using Advanced Technology documents obtained from open court files in *Church of Scientology v. Fishman,* 1994 WL 467999 (9th Cir.1994); finding fair use defense exists where no separate market for works because Scientologists cannot effectively use them without the Church's supervision);

*F.A.C.T.NET,*https://apps.fastcase.com/Research/Pages/Document.
aspx?LTID=v%2b%2bWn0pFJOPwVn7bDpURwR5rY%2bXX9U
ta8hAwg5stZDj8sEobQkSQ%2bky70Tw1SszD6GuoylZ859kfbr0
CHnkdXRmwxLW7cJtCJym88GmTgsrrExWnNNSNiN61CAkvo 365&ECF=901+F.Supp.+at+1524- 26 901 F.Supp. at 1524-26

(denying preliminary injunction against copying of Advanced Technology works based on fair use defense because financial harm to the Church was unlikely, there was no commercial motive, works were used in part of "ongoing dialogue" on the Internet, and there was no showing of a potential effect on the market for plaintiffs' works).

4. Conclusion

Accordingly, plaintiffs have demonstrated a likelihood of success on its claims that Erlich infringed their copyrights on all of the Exhibit A and B works, except items 4 and 9 of Exhibit A and item 9 of Exhibit B.

C. Likelihood of Success on Trade Secret Claim

In the third cause of action, plaintiff RTC alleges that Erlich misappropriated its trade secrets. California has adopted a version of the Uniform Trade Secret Act ("UTSA"), Cal.Civ.Code § 3426.1 et seq. The UTSA defines a trade secret as information, including a formula, pattern, compilation, program, device, method, technique, or process, that:

(1) Derives independent economic value, actual or potential, from not being generally known to the public or to other persons who can obtain economic value from its disclosure or use; and

(2) Is the subject of efforts that are reasonable under the circumstances to maintain its secrecy.

Cal.Civ.Code § 3426.1(d).[21] The UTSA further defines "misappropriation" of a trade secret as

(1) Acquisition of a trade secret of another by a person who knows or has reason to know that the trade secret was acquired by improper means; or

(2) Disclosure or use of a trade secret of another without express or implied consent by a person who:

(A) Used improper means to acquire knowledge of the trade secret; or

(B) (B). At the time of disclosure or use, knew or had reason to know that his or her knowledge of the trade secret was:

i. Derived from or through a person who had utilized improper means to acquire it;

ii. Acquired under circumstances giving rise to a duty to maintain its secrecy or limit its use; or

iii. Derived from or through a person who owed a duty to the person seeking relief to maintain its secrecy or limit its use; or

(C). Before a material change of his or her position, knew or had reason to know that it was a trade secret and that knowledge of it had been acquired by accident or mistake.

Id. § 3426.1(b).

To establish its trade secret claim, RTC must show, *inter alia,* that the Advanced Technology works (1) have independent economic

Page 1251

value to competitors and (2) have been kept confidential.

1. Nature of Works

As a preliminary matter, Erlich argues that the Advanced Technology works cannot be trade secrets because of their nature as religious scriptures. In *Wollersheim,*https://apps.fastcase.com /Research/Pages/Document.aspx?LTI D=v%2b%2bWn0pFJOPwV n7bDpURwR5rY%2bXX9Uta8hAwg5stZDj8s EobQkSQ%2bky7 0Tw1SszD6GuoylZ859kfbr0CHnkdXRmwxLW7cJtCJy m88Gm TgsrrExWnNNSNiN61CAkvo365&ECF=796+F.2d+at+ 1090-91 796 F.2d at 1090-91, the Ninth Circuit rejected the Church's application for a preliminary injunction on the basis of a trade secret claim against a splinter Scientology group that had acquired stolen copies of the Advanced Technology. The Church argued not that the works gave them a competitive market advantage but that disclosure of the works would cause its adherents "religious harm ... from premature unsupervised exposure to the materials." *Id.* Although the Ninth Circuit rejected plaintiffs' trade secret argument based on the *spiritual* value of the harm, it later noted that it had left open the question of whether the Advanced Technology works could qualify as trade secrets, assuming plaintiffs could prove that the secrets confer on them an actual *economic* advantage over competitors.

Religious Center v. Scott, 869 F.2d 1306, 1310 (9th Cir.1989); *cf.* *Vien,*https://apps.fastcase.com/Research/Pages/Document.aspx?LT ID=v%2b%2bWn0pFJOPwVn7bDpURwR5rY%2bXX9Uta8hAw g5stZDj8sEobQkSQ%2bky70Tw1SszD6GuoylZ859kfbr0CHnkdX RmwxLW7cJtCJym88GmTgsrrExWnNNSNiN61CAkvo365&EC F=827+F.Supp.+at+629 827 F.Supp. at 629.[22] Nonetheless, the court noted that such an allegation would "raise grave doubts about [the Church's] claim as a religion and a not-for- profit corporation."[23] *Id.* (quoting *Wollersheim,*https://apps.fastcase.com/

Research/Pages/Document.aspx?LTI
D=v%2b%2bWn0pFJOPwV
n7bDpURwR5rY%2bXX9Uta8hAwg5stZDj8sEobQkS
Q%2bky70
Tw1SszD6GuoylZ859kfbr0CHnkdXRmwxLW7cJtCJy
m88GmTgs
rrExWnNNSNiN61CAkvo365&ECF=796+F.2d+at+109
1 796 F.2d at 1091).

The Church contends that the Advanced Technology works consist of "*processes* and the theory behind those processes ... that are to be used precisely as set forth by L. Ron Hubbard to assist the parishioner in achieving a greater spiritual awareness and freedom." McShane February 27, 1995 Decl. ¶ 9 (emphasis added). Erlich responds that the works are essentially religious texts. *Cf.* FAC ¶ 9 (describing Hubbard as author of "applied religious philosophy and spiritual healing technology" and works as "training materials and course manuals of the Scientology religion").

Erlich argues that the Church cannot have trade secrets because trade secret law is necessarily related to commerce. *See Kewanee Oil Co. v. Bicron Corp.,* 416 U.S. 470, 481, 485, 94 S.Ct. 1879,

1886, 1888, 40 L.Ed.2d 315(1974). The Church contends that, like other organizations, it must pay bills, and that licensing fees from these documents allow it to continue operating. McShane February 27, 1995 Decl.7.

The Church's status as a religion does not itself preclude it from holding a trade secret. Restatement § 39 cmt. d, at 429 ("[N]onprofit entities such as ... religious organizations can also claim trade secret protection for economically valuable information such as lists of prospective members or donors."); UTSA § 3426.1(c) (defining "person" to include a "corporation ... or any other legal or commercial entity"); *cf.*

United Christian Scientists v. Christian Science Board of Directors, 829 F.2d 1152, 1169 (D.C.Cir.1987) (noting that Church was entitled to copyright protection on same basis as nonreligious groups). With the exception of the *Vien* case, there is little authority to support a finding that religious materials can constitute trade secrets. However, there is "no category of information [that] is excluded from protection as a trade secret because of its inherent qualities." *Clark v. Bunker,* 453 F.2d 1006, 1009 (9th Cir.1972) (citing Restatement of Torts, § 757 cmt. b, at 5) (upholding as a trade secret a "detailed plan for the creation, promotion, financing, and sale of contracts for `prepaid' or `pre-need' funeral services"); *see also Smith v. Dravo*

Page 1252

*Corp.,*https://apps.fastcase.com/Research/Pages/Document.aspx?LTID=v%2b%2bWn0pFJOPwVn7bDpURwR5rY%2bXX9Uta8hAwg5stZDj8sEobQkSQ%2bky70Tw1SszD6GuoylZ859kfbr0CHnkdXRmwxLW7cJtCJym88GmTgsrrExWnNNSNiN61CAkvo365&ECF=203+F.2d+369%2c+373+%287th+Cir.1953%29 203 F.2d 369,

373 (7th Cir.1953) ("We assume that almost any knowledge or information used in the conduct of one's business may be held by its possessor in secret.").

Nor is there any authority to support Erlich's argument that the Church's religious texts cannot be trade secrets because, unlike most trade secrets, these secrets are not *used* in the production or sales of a commodity but *are the commodities themselves.* The Church's Advanced Technology "course" materials, which are an integral part of the Church's spiritual counseling techniques, do not appear fundamentally different from the course manuals upheld as trade secrets in *SmokEnders, Inc. v. Smoke No More, Inc.*, 184 U.S.P.Q. 309 (S.D.Fla. 1974):

> The [SmokEnders ("SE")] program requires attendees to follow a rigid structured regimen comprised of specific assignments and detail[ed] concepts as recited in [the manual]....
>
> The SE program is a step-by-step regimented program which requires that each person attending a SE program perform each act of the program at a particular time. Each act required by a SE seminar attendee must be performed by attendees at the same time in the program, with each a minimum departure from the program.

The SE trade secret resides in the composite program as it is arranged for step-by-step delivery to the attendees.

Id. at 312 (emphasis added). *SmokEnders* is arguably distinguishable because only the "moderators" and not the attendees were given access to the course materials in that case. However, the adherents of the Church, unlike the attendees and like the moderators in *SmokEnders,* are under a duty of confidentiality as to the materials. This case is analogous to *SmokEnders* because in both cases the "commodity" that is produced from the trade secrets is the result achieved by the person using the course materials and their techniques (whether it be stopping smoking or reaching a "higher spiritual existence").

Thus, there is at least some precedent for granting trade secret status to works that are techniques for improving oneself (though not specifically spiritually). Conversely, there is no authority for excluding religious materials from trade secret protection because of their nature. Indeed, there is no authority for excluding any type of information because of its nature. While the trade secret laws did not necessarily develop to allow a religion to protect a monopoly in its religious practices, the laws have nonetheless expanded such that the Church's techniques, which clearly are "used in the operation of the enterprise," Restatement § 39, at 425, are deserving of protection if secret and valuable.

Although trade secret status may apply to works that are techniques for spiritually improving oneself, the secret aspect of those techniques must be defined with particularity. *See* Restatement § 39 cmt. d, at 430 (requiring plaintiff to define the information claimed as a trade secret with sufficient definiteness). It appears that plaintiffs are claiming that the entire works themselves, which they describe as "processes and the theory behind those processes," constitute the trade secrets. *See* Pltfs.' Mem. in Support of Prelim.Inj. at 17. This definition is problematic because it is impossible to determine when the "secret" has been lost after portions of the works have been disclosed. *Cf.*

*F.A.C.T.NET,*https://apps.fastcase.com/Research/Pages/Document. aspx?LTID=v%2b%2bWn0pFJOPwVn7bDpURwR5rY%2bXX9

Uta8hAw
g5stZDj8sEobQkSQ%2bky70Tw1SszD6GuoylZ859kfb
r0CHnkdX
RmwxLW7cJtCJym88GmTgsrrExWnNNSNiN61CAkv
o365&EC F=901+F.Supp.+at+1527 901 F.Supp. at 1527 ("In the course of the hearing ... RTC changed its position with regard to what materials constitute the purported trade secrets."). Although plaintiffs' definition has at least some support in *SmokEnders,* where the court upheld as a trade secret a "composite [stop- smoking] program" found in an instructional manual, 184 U.S.P.Q. at 312, this court is not satisfied that plaintiffs have identified their trade secrets with sufficient definiteness to support injunctive relief.

2. Independent Economic Value

A trade secret requires proof of "independent economic value, actual or potential, from not being generally known to the public or to other persons who can obtain economic value from its disclosure or use." UTSA

§ 3426.1(d)(1). A trade secret must Page 1253 have sufficient value in the owner's operation of its enterprise such that it provides an actual or potential advantage over others who do not possess the information. Restatement § 39 cmt. e, at 430.

RTC's president, Warren McShane, attests that [t]he Advanced Technology is a source of substantial revenue for RTC in the form of licensing fees paid by Churches that are licensed to use the Advanced Technology. These Churches themselves receive a significant amount of their income from donations by parishioners for services based upon the Advanced Technology. These Churches pay RTC a percentage of the donations paid by parishioners for the services based upon the Advanced Technology. These donations and fees provide the majority of operating expenses of these various Church organizations.

McShane May 31, 1995 Decl. 16; *see also Vien*,https://apps.fastcase.com/Research/Pages/Document.aspx?LT ID=v%2b%2bWn0pFJOPwVn7bDpURwR5rY%2bXX9Uta8hAw g5stZDj8sEobQkSQ%2bky70Tw1SszD6GuoylZ859kfbr0CHnkdX RmwxLW7cJtCJym88GmTgsrrExWnNNSNiN61CAkv o365&EC F=827+F.Supp.+at+633 827 F.Supp. at 633 (finding Advanced Technology has value to Church by helping support its operations world-wide). The Church's need for revenues to support its services is no less because of its status as a religion. *Id.* (citing *Murdock v. Commonwealth of Pennsylvania,* 319 U.S. 105, 111, 63 S.Ct. 870,

874, 87 L.Ed. 1292 (1943)). RTC points out that it receives six percent of what the individual churches receive in licensing fees. J. Kobrin May 31, 1995 Decl, Ex. A ("McShane Depo."), at 43. This evidence is sufficient to establish the value of the Advanced Technology works to the Church.

Erlich also argues that, to constitute a trade secret, information must give its owner a *competitive* advantage, which implies that the Church must have competitors, as it did in *Vien. See Ruckelshaus v. Monsanto Co.,* 467 U.S. 986, 1011 n. 15, 104 S.Ct. 2862, 2877 n.

15, 81 L.Ed.2d 815 (1984);

ABBA Rubber Co. v. Seaquist, 235 Cal. App.3d 1, 18, 286 Cal.Rptr. 518 (1991). Although Erlich is clearly not a "competitor" of the Church, there is no requirement that a trade secret have any value to the *defendant;* the value can be to *others* who do not possess it. Rest.

§ 39 cmt. e, at 430. The Church has admitted, however, that it currently has no "competitors." McShane Depo. at 95. However, the definition of trade secret does not require that there *currently* be competitors, only that there be actual or *potential* value from the information being secret. Thus, potential competition is sufficient. *Id.* This evidence can be shown by direct evidence of the impact of the information on the business or by circumstantial evidence of the resources invested in producing the information, the precautions taken to protect its secrecy, and the willingness of others to pay for its access. Restatement § 39 cmt. e, at 431. The several past instances of breakaway Scientology-like groups exploiting RTC's Advanced Technology works for their profit constitute reasonable circumstantial evidence that these works give the Church a competitive advantage. *See* McShane Depo. at 93-94 (citing several former Church members who started rival factions);

*Vien,*https://apps.fastcase.com/Research/Pages/Document.aspx?LTID=v%2b%2bWn0pFJOPwVn7bDpURwR5rY%2bXX9Uta8hAwg5stZDj8sEobQkSQ%2bky70Tw1SszD6GuoylZ859kfbr0CHnkdXRmwxLW7cJtCJym88GmTgsrrExWnNNSNiN61CAkvo365&EC F=827+F.Supp.+at+634 827 F.Supp. at 634 (describing a rival faction);*Wollersheim,*https://apps.fastcase.com/Research/Pages/Document.aspx?LTID=v%2b%2bWn0pFJOPwVn7bDpURwR5rY%2bXX9Uta8hAwg5stZDj8sEobQkSQ%2bky70Tw1SszD6GuoylZ859kfbr0CHnkdXRmwxLW7cJtCJym88GmTgsrrExWnNNSNiN61 CAkvo365&ECF=796+F.2d+at+1078 796

F.2d at 1078 (same). In fact, McShane's declaration constitutes direct evidence that the works have a significant impact on the donations received by the Church, providing a majority of its operating expenses. McShane May 31, 1995 Decl. ¶ 16. The status of the Advanced Technology works as trade secrets should not depend on Erlich's use of them. Accordingly, this court finds support for the court's conclusion in *Vien* that the Church has shown independent economic value.

3. Secrecy

Information is protectable as a trade secret where the owner has taken "efforts that are *reasonable* under the circumstances to maintain its secrecy." UTSA § 3426.1(d)(2) (emphasis added). "Reasonable efforts" can include advising employees of the existence of a trade secret, limiting access to the information on a "need to know basis," *Courtesy Temporary Service, Inc. v.*

Camacho, 222 Cal.App.3d 1278, 1288, 272 Cal.Rptr. 352 (1990), requiring employees to sign confidentiality agreements, *MAI Systems Corp. v. Peak Computer*, 991 F.2d 511, 521 (9th Cir.1993), and keeping secret documents under lock, 1 Milgrim § 1.04, at 1-

126. *Accord* Restatement § 39 cmt. g, at 435. The court finds that RTC has put forward

Page 1254

sufficient evidence that it took steps that were reasonable under the circumstances to protect its purported trade secrets. RTC's president describes elaborate means taken to ensure the confidentiality of the Advanced Technology works, including use of locked cabinets, safes, logging and identification of the materials, availability of the materials at only a handful of sites worldwide, electronic sensors attached to documents, locked briefcases for transporting works, alarms, photo identifications, security personnel, and confidentiality agreements for all of those given access to the materials. McShane February 8, 1995 Decl. 13-18. McShane testifies that all copies of the Advanced Technology works that are outside of the Church were gained through improper means, such as by theft. *Id.* 22-24. Thirty- five other declarants confirm that the measures mentioned by McShane have been used, though not in exactly the same manner, in other Churches and at other times. *See e.g.,* Sydejko Decl. (describing measures used at Erlich's facilities during relevant time period); Byrne Decl. ¶ 15 (stating works have been kept confidential since at least 1968). There is further evidence that Erlich himself signed confidentiality agreements with respect to the Advanced Technology materials and, specifically, the upper-level "NOTS" course materials. *See* McShane February 8, 1995 Decl., Exs. H-I; McShane February 27, 1995 Decl., Exs. D-F; McShane Depo. at 201-03; H. Kobrin Mary 31, 1995 Decl., Ex. A ("Erlich Depo."), at 84-88. The court is unpersuaded by Erlich's claims that the Church's measures have not covered all locations where the Advanced

Technology works are found and do not cover crucial time periods.[24] Efforts at maintaining secrecy need not be extreme, just reasonable under the circumstances. Legislative Committee Comment — Senate, Cal.Civ.Code § 3426.1, at 147 (West Supp.1995). The Church has made more than an adequate showing on this issue.[25]

Erlich raises a number of objections to the Church's claims of confidentiality. Erlich argues that the Church's trade secrets have been made available to the public through various means. The unprotected disclosure of a trade secret will cause the information to forfeit its trade secret status, since "[i]nformation that is generally known or readily ascertainable through proper means by others ... is not protectable as a trade secret." Restatement § 39 cmt. f, at 432; *see also* Cal.Civ.Code § 3426.1(d); *Kewanee Oil,*https://apps.fastcase.com/Research/Pages/Document.aspx?LTI D=v%2b%2bWn0pFJOPwVn7bDpURwR5rY%2bXX9 Uta8hAwg 5stZDj8sEobQkSQ%2bky70Tw1SszD6GuoylZ859kfbr 0CHnkdX RmwxLW7cJtCJym88GmTgsrrExWnNNSNiN61CAkv o365&EC F=416+U.S.+at+484 416 U.S. at 484, 94 S.Ct. at 1887; *Chicago*

Lock Co. v. Fanberg, 676 F.2d 400, 404 (9th Cir.1982); 1 Milgrim at 1-135. Once trade secrets have been exposed to the public, they cannot later be recalled. *In re Remington Arms Co.,*https://apps.fastcase.com/Research/Pages/Document.aspx?LTI D=v%2b%2bWn0pFJOPwVn7bDpURwR5rY%2bXX9 Uta8hAwg 5stZDj8sEobQkSQ%2bky70Tw1SszD6GuoylZ859kfbr 0CHnkdX RmwxLW7cJtCJym88GmTgsrrExWnNNSNiN61CAkv o365&EC F=952+F.2d+1029%2c+1033+%28 8th+Cir.1991%29 952 F.2d 1029, 1033 (8th Cir.1991);

*Smith,*https://apps.fastcase.com/Research/Pages/Document.aspx?LTID=v%2b%2bWn0pFJOPwVn7bDpURwR5rY%2bXX9Uta8hAwg5stZDj8sEobQkSQ%2bky70Tw1SszD6GuoylZ859kfbr0CHnkdXRmwxLW7cJtCJym88GmTgsrrExWnNNSNiN61CAkvo365&ECF=203+F.2d+at+373 203 F.2d at 373.

Erlich argues that many of the Advanced Technology documents have been available in open court records in another case, *Church of Scientology Int'l v. Fishman,* Case No. 91-6426 HLH (C.D.Cal.), destroying the necessary element of secrecy. *Cf.*

*Lerma,*https://apps.fastcase.com/Research/Pages/Document.aspx?LTID=v%2b%2bWn0pFJOPwVn7bDpURwR5rY%2bXX9Uta8hAwg5stZDj8sEobQkSQ%2bky70Tw1SszD6GuoylZ859kfbr0CHnkdXRmwxLW7cJtCJym88GmTgsrrExWnNNSNiN61CAkvo365&ECF=897+F.Supp.+at+262 897 F.Supp. at 262 (noting that some of Advanced Technology works were available in the court file in *Fishman* and that they were not subject to a sealing or protective

Page 1255

order). However, the *Fishman* court recently issued an order sealing the file pending a decision on whether the documents are trade secrets. Even if those records were temporarily open to the public, the court will not assume that their contents have been generally disclosed, especially when this question is still pending before the district court in *Fishman.* Such a disclosure, without evidence that the secrets have become generally known, does not necessarily cause RTC to forfeit its trade secrets. *See Gates Rubber Co. v. Bando Chemical Industries, Ltd.,* 9 F.3d 823, 848-49 (10th Cir.1993) (finding that information retained its secret status despite being disclosed at hearing, where plaintiff evidenced continuing intent to maintain its secrecy by acting to seal the record). The contrary result would mean that if documents were ever filed without a sealing order, even for a short time, the court would not be able to decide that they should be sealed because the documents would have lost their potential trade secret status by virtue of the temporary unsealing. The only fair result would be to allow trade secret status for works that are otherwise protectable as trade secrets unless they were somehow made generally available to the public during the period they were unsealed, such as by publication.

Erlich further asserts that the Advanced Technology has been largely disclosed in the popular press, as evidenced by various publications attached to the Berger Declaration, which was originally filed in the *Fishman* case.[26] These articles may reveal information referring to or hinting at the trade secrets, but may not disclose the secrets themselves, *see* McShane May 31, 1995 Decl. 12 (cataloging what was disclosed by the Exhibits in *Fishman*).[27] However, as previously noted, the court is not certain how to properly define the "secrets." To the extent that someone uses or discloses any information taken from any of these articles, there is clearly no trade secret claim. However, much of Erlich's postings copied all or almost all of sections of the Advanced Technology works, which is far more than has ever been disclosed in the popular press. *See id.* 12-15. In fact, several of the works posted by Erlich are not mentioned in any of the clippings in the Berger declaration. *Id.* Arguably, the Church's alleged secrets are such that their value depends on the availability of the complete courses and not mere fragments, thus disclosures that describe parts of the works or disclose isolated portions do not necessarily suffice to ruin the value of the entire works as secrets. *Cf.*

*SmokEnders,*https://apps.fastcase.com/Research/Pages/Document.aspx?LTID=v%2b%2bWn0pFJOPwVn7bDpURwR5rY%2bXX9Uta8hAwg5stZDj8sEobQkSQ%2bky70Tw1SszD6GuoylZ859kfbr0CHnkdXRmwxLW7cJtCJym88GmTgsrrExWnNNSNiN61CAkvo36 5&ECF=184+U.S.P.Q.+at+317184 U.S.P.Q. at 317 (finding that secret's value can be from unified design including components that are individually in the public domain). However, without a clearer definition of what constitute the "secrets," the court is unable to determine whether some have been made generally known to the public.[28]

Finally, Erlich newly emphasizes in his Reply that the works he posted were not secrets because he received them through proper means: eight of the documents were allegedly previously posted anonymously to a public portion of the Internet and one of the

Page 1256

documents (item 1 of Exhibit B) allegedly came to Erlich anonymously through the U.S. mail. Erlich claims that because the alleged trade secrets were received from "public sources," they should lose their trade secret protection. Although the Internet is a new technology, it requires no great leap to conclude that because more than 25 million people could have accessed the newsgroup postings from which Erlich alleges he received the Exhibit B works, these works would lose their status as secrets. While the Internet has not reached the status where a temporary posting on a newsgroup is akin to publication in a major newspaper or on a television network, those with an interest in using the Church's trade secrets to compete with the Church are likely to look to the newsgroup. Thus, posting works to the Internet makes them "generally known" to the relevant people— the potential "competitors" of the Church.

The court is troubled by the notion that any Internet user, including those using "anonymous remailers"[29] to protect their identity, can destroy valuable intellectual property rights by posting them over the Internet, especially given the fact that there is little opportunity to screen postings before they are made. *See* Eduardo M. Carreras, "Intellectual Property: First Casualty on the Information Highway," 13 No. 1 ACCA Docket 26 (Westlaw) ("Carreras") (Jan.-Feb. 1995) at *29-*32 (suggesting that trade secret protection is lost as soon as information is disclosed on the Internet). Nonetheless, one of the Internet's virtues, that it gives even the poorest individuals the power to publish to millions of readers, *see* Eugene Volokh, "Cheap Speech and What It Will Do," 104 Yale L.J. 1805, 1806-07 (1995), can also be a detriment to the value of intellectual property rights. The anonymous (or judgment proof) defendant can permanently destroy valuable trade secrets, leaving no one to hold liable for the misappropriation. *See* Carreras at *30. Although a work posted to an

Internet newsgroup remains accessible to the public for only a limited amount of time, once that trade secret has been released into the public domain there is no retrieving it. *In re Remington*

*Arms,*https://apps.fastcase.com/Research/Pages/Document.aspx?LTID=v%2b%2bWn0pFJOPwVn7bDpURwR5rY%2bXX9Uta8hAwg5stZDj8sEobQkSQ%2bky70Tw1SszD6Guoy1Z859kfbr0CHnkdXRmwxLW7cJtCJym88GmTgsrrExWnNNSNiN61CAkvo365&ECF=952+F.2d+at+1033 952 F.2d at 1033. While the court is persuaded by the Church's evidence that those who made the original postings likely gained the information through improper means, as no one outside the Church or without a duty of confidence would have had access to those works,[30] this does not negate the finding that, once posted, the works lost their secrecy. Although Erlich cannot rely on his own improper postings to support the argument that the Church's documents are no longer secrets, *see* 3 Milgrim § 15.01[1][a][ii], at 15-43, evidence that another individual has put the alleged trade secrets into the public domain prevents RTC from further enforcing its trade secret rights in those materials. Because there is no evidence that Erlich is a privy of any of the alleged original misappropriators, he is not equitably estopped from raising their previous public disclosures as a defense to his disclosure. *Underwater Storage, Inc. v. United States Rubber Co.,* 371 F.2d 950, 955 (D.C.Cir.1966), *cert.*

*denied,*https://apps.fastcase.com/Research/Pages/Document.aspx?LTID=v%2b%2bWn0pFJOPwVn7bDpURwR5rY%2bXX9Uta8hAwg5stZDj8sEobQkSQ%2bky70Tw1SszD6GuoylZ859kfbr0CHnkdXRmwxLW7cJtCJym88GmTgsrrExWnNNSNiN61CAkvo365& ECF=386+U.S.+911 386 U.S. 911, 87 S.Ct. 859, 17 L.Ed.2d 784 (1967) ("Once the secret is out, the rest of the world may well have a right to copy it at will; but this should not protect the misappropriator or his privies."). The court is thus convinced that those postings made by Erlich were of materials that were possibly already generally available to the public. *See*

*Lerma,*https://apps.fastcase.com/Research/Pages/Document.aspx?LTID=v%2b%2bWn0pFJOPwVn7bDpURwR5rY%2bXX9Uta8hAwg5stZDj8sEobQkSQ%2bky70Tw1SszD6GuoylZ859kfbr0CHnkdXRmwxLW7cJtCJym88GmTgsrrExWnNNSNiN61CAkvo365&ECF=897+F.Supp.+at+266 897 F.Supp. at 266 (finding that RTC could not show the

Page 1257

Advanced Technology works were not "generally known" to support injunctive relief);

*F.A.C.T.NET,*https://apps.fastcase.com/Research/Pages/Document.aspx?LTID=v%2b%2bWn0pFJOPwVn7bDpURwR5rY%2bXX9Uta8hAwg5stZDj8sEobQkSQ%2bky70Tw1SszD6GuoylZ859kfbr0CHnkdXRmwxLW7cJtCJym88GmTgsrrExWnNNSNiN61CAkvo365&ECF=901+F.Supp.+at+1527 901 F.Supp. at 1527 (same). Therefore, RTC has not shown a likelihood of success on an essential element of its trade secret claim.[31]

4. Conclusion and Alternative Test

Because RTC is the plaintiff, and because it is moving for injunctive relief, it bears the burden of proving its trade secrets. 3 Milgrim § 15.01[1]. The court finds that RTC has failed to adequately define its trade secrets and, at least as to those works that have been made available to the public through previous Internet postings not by Erlich, RTC has failed to meet its burden on the issue of secrecy. Therefore, RTC has failed to show a likelihood of success on its trade secret misappropriation claim.

RTC's failure to prove a likelihood of success on its trade secret claim of secrecy does not necessarily preclude it from showing an entitlement to a preliminary injunction. RTC can meet the second formulation of the preliminary injunction test by showing a combination of serious questions going to the merits of its trade secret claim and that the balance of hardships tips in its favor. However, since the trade secrets have not been adequately defined, the court cannot find that serious questions going to the merits have been sufficiently raised to justify a preliminary injunction on the trade secret claim. Until RTC better describes what its trade secrets are, it is impossible to determine whether previous public disclosures of parts of the Advanced Technology works are sufficient to destroy the secrecy of the entire work. While *parts* of many of the works have been mentioned in various published articles and books, the court is unclear what effect such disclosures would have on the secrecy and value of an *entire* work. The court is also not entirely persuaded by RTC's argument that its secrets have competitive value to future breakaway groups. These issues will have to be resolved before RTC can ultimately prevail on its trade secret claims.

D. Irreparable Injury and Balance of Hardships

The court will presume irreparable harm for the copyright claim because plaintiffs have shown a likelihood of success on their claims of infringement. *Johnson Controls, Inc. v. Phoenix Control Systems, Inc.,* 886 F.2d 1173, 1174 (9th Cir.1989); *Apple Computer, Inc. v. Formula International, Inc.,* 725 F.2d 521 (9th Cir.1984).

E. First Amendment Concerns

In his Reply, Erlich argues that there is a strong presumption against any

Page 1258

injunction that could act as a "prior restraint" on free speech, citing

CBS, Inc. v. Davis, U.S. , 114 S.Ct. 912, 913-14, 127

L.Ed.2d358 (1994) (Justice Blackmun, as Circuit Justice, staying a preliminary injunction prohibiting CBS from airing footage from inside meat packing plant). The court notes, however, that the 1976 Act explicitly sanctions the use of preliminary injunctions in the case of copyright infringement. 17 U.S.C. §§ 501(a), 502(a). The Supreme Court has recognized that the Copyright Act itself embodies a balance between the rights of copyright holders, guaranteed by the Constitution, U.S. Const. art. I, § 8, and the protections of the First Amendment. *See Harper &*

*Row,*https://apps.fastcase.com/Research/Pages/Document.aspx?LT

ID=v%2b%2bWn0pFJOPwVn7bDpURwR5rY%2bXX9

Uta8hAw

g5stZDj8sEobQkSQ%2bky70Tw1SszD6GuoylZ859kfb

r0CHnkdX RmwxLW7cJtCJym88GmTgsrrExWnNNSNiN61CAkvo365&EC F=471+U.S.+at+557-60 471 U.S. at 557-60, 105 S.Ct. at 2229-30;

*In re Capital Cities/ABC, Inc,*https://apps.fastcase.com

/Research/Pages/Document.aspx?LTID=v%2b%2bWn0pFJOPwV n7bDpURwR5rY%2bXX9Uta8hAwg5stZDj8sEobQkSQ%2bky70 Tw1SszD6GuoylZ859kfbr0CHnkdXRmwxLW7cJtCJym88GmTgs rrExWnNNSNiN61CAkvo365&ECF=918+F.2d+140%2c+143- 44+%2811th+Cir.1990%29 918 F.2d 140, 143-44 (11th Cir.1990).

The doctrine of fair use already considers First Amendment concerns. *New Era Publications International, ApS v. Henry Holt & Co.,* 873 F.2d 576, 584 (2d Cir.1989), *cert.*

*denied,*https://apps.fastcase.com/Research/Pages/Document.aspx? LTID=v%2b%2bWn0pFJOPwVn7bDpURwR5rY%2bXX9Uta8h

Awg5stZDj8sEobQkSQ%2bky70Tw1SszD6GuoylZ859 kfbr0CHn kdXRmwxLW7cJtCJym88GmTgsrrExWnNNSNiN61C Akvo365& ECF=493+U.S.+1094 493 U.S.1094, 110 S.Ct. 1168, 107 L.Ed.2d

1071 (1990) (rejecting defendant's argument that First Amendment concerns precluded granting an injunction, though finding other equitable considerations dictated denial of injunctive relief). Because Erlich is able to continue to criticize the Church and use its published and unpublished works to the extent allowed by the doctrine of fair use and because the injunctive relief sought is no broader than necessary to protect plaintiffs' copyrights, Erlich's First Amendment interests have been adequately considered.

F. Conclusion

Plaintiffs have shown a likelihood of success on the merits of their copyright claims except as to item 4 of Exhibit A, for which the copyright has expired. Plaintiffs gain the benefit of a presumption of irreparable harm as to this claim. Accordingly, plaintiffs are entitled to a preliminary injunction prohibiting any further copying of plaintiffs' copyrighted Exhibit A and B works pending a trial on the merits, except as to item 4 of Exhibit A and as allowed by the doctrine of fair use.[32] Under the fair use doctrine, Erlich may post, or otherwise publish, his criticism of the Church, using plaintiffs' copyrighted Exhibit A and B works to the extent necessary to carry out his critical purpose. However, the court notes that copying the works in their entirety with very little added criticism is almost certainly not fair use.

Accordingly, the court grants in part and denies in part plaintiffs' application for a preliminary injunction and Erlich's motion to dissolve the TRO.

III. PLAINTIFFS' APPLICATION TO EXPAND THE TRO

Plaintiffs have applied to expand the scope of the preliminary injunction against Erlich to include more of plaintiffs' works that are allegedly protected by copyright and trade secret law, beyond those listed in Exhibits A and B of the FAC. This request comes after plaintiffs maintain that Erlich violated a promise he made to the court to convince it to continue the contempt hearing. On March 14, 1995, counsel for Erlich stated that Erlich "would agree not to publish any of Mr. Ron Hubbard's writings, or copyright-registered writings of the Church of Scientology, until the contempt hearing." *See* March 16, 1995 Order Setting Hearing Dates. Plaintiffs seek to expand the number of documents covered by the injunction to include 52 works because Erlich allegedly "furnished a copy of another copyrighted, confidential work, taken from the same course as the document which he posted in his first violation of the TRO, to a litigant in another lawsuit." Ex Parte App. for Amended TRO at

4. However, plaintiffs have not provided Erlich or the court with the registrations for these materials to allow a determination that they are the subject of valid copyright interests. The scope of this case should not be expanded to encompass all or a large number of Hubbard's copyrighted works merely because Erlich made a promise to allow the postponement of the contempt hearing. Now that there has been a contempt hearing, and

Page 1259

given the court's finding that Erlich was not in contempt, *see* part IV *infra,* the court does not believe that an overly expansive preliminary injunction is appropriate. In fact, a broad injunction which goes beyond the scope of the allegedly infringing activities should be avoided for First Amendment reasons. *See* 3 Nimmer § 14.06[C], at 14-106 to -109 (noting that scope of injunction should be coterminous with, and no broader than, infringement); *In re Capital Cities/ABC, Inc.,*https://apps.fastcase.com/Research

/Pages/Document.aspx?LTID=v%2b%2bWn0pFJO PwVn7bDpUR wR5rY%2bXX9Uta8hAwg5stZDj8sEobQkSQ%2bky70 Tw1SszD 6GuoylZ859kfbr0CHnkdXRmwxLW7cJtCJym88GmT gsrrExWnN NSNiN61CAkvo365&ECF=918+F.2d+at+144 918 F.2d at 144 (calling for a "surgical" restraint to accommodate First Amendment rights). Accordingly, the court denies plaintiffs' application for an expansion of the injunctive relief.[33]

Request To Seize Erlich's Computer

The court finds plaintiffs' request that Erlich's computer and other equipment be seized to be wholly without merit. No amount of excessive copying in the context of criticism, which is potentially subject to a valid fair use defense, would warrant such a seizure. Here, Erlich's equipment is hardly an instrument of infringement. Rather, it is essential to the operation of his business and other affairs. While a specifically-tailored injunction in a copyright case does not offend the First Amendment, attempting to shut down a critic's speech activities, including those that do not implicate the copyright laws in the least, would constitute an unwarranted prior restraint on speech. *Cf.* 3 Nimmer § 14.06[C], at 14-107 to -109; *RCA Records v.*

All-Fast Systems, Inc., 594 F.Supp. 335, 340 (S.D.N.Y.1984) (where action not against record pirates, court should not seize equipment which can be used for non-infringing purposes).

IV. MOTION FOR CONTEMPT

The Ninth Circuit set forth the standards for civil contempt in *In re Dual-Deck Video Cassette Antitrust*

*Litigation,*https://apps.fast case.com/Research/Pages/Document.aspx?LTID=v%2 b%2bWn0p FJOPwVn7bDpURwR5rY%2bXX9Uta8hAwg5stZDj8s EobQkSQ

%2bky70Tw1SszD6GuoylZ859kfbr0CHnkdXRmw xLW7cJtCJym 88GmTgsrrExWnNNSNiN61CAkvo365&ECF=10+F.3d +693+%2

89th+Ci r.1993%29 10 F.3d 693 (9th Cir.1993):

Civil contempt in this context consists of a party's disobedience to a specific and definite court order by failure to take all reasonable steps within the party's power to comply. The contempt "need not be willful," and there is no good faith exception to the requirement of obedience to a court order. But a person should not be held in contempt if his action "`appears to be based on a good faith and reasonable interpretation of the [court's order].'" "Substantial compliance" with the court order is a defense to civil contempt, and is not vitiated by "a few technical violations" where every reasonable effort has been made to comply.

The party alleging civil contempt must demonstrate that the alleged contemnor violated the court's order by "clear and convincing evidence," not merely a preponderance of the evidence....

This set of rules is easy to articulate but difficult to apply. [The court must properly determine] (1) that [plaintiff] violated the court order,

(2) beyond substantial compliance, (3) not based on a good faith and reasonable interpretation of the order, (4) by clear and convincing evidence.

Id. at 695 (citations omitted). Plaintiffs allege that Erlich has violated the terms of the Amended TRO on three separate occasions.

A. First Alleged Contempt

First, plaintiffs allege that Erlich was in contempt of this court's February 10, 1995 TRO or its February 23, 1995 Amended TRO when, on February 26, 1995, Erlich posted portions of item 1 of Exhibit B, the Class VIII "Assists" tape transcript ("the Assists transcript"). Erlich contends that he had not received the court's Amended TRO at the time he made the posting. At the time of the posting, Erlich was not yet represented by counsel. The court's original TRO enjoined Erlich from making certain uses of the Exhibit A and B works, but did not make clear that Erlich could make fair use of the non-trade secret Exhibit A works. From the content of Erlich's posting, it seems that

Page 1260

Erlich thought he was engaging in fair use of the Assists transcript. While the court did not explicitly indicate that Erlich could make "fair use" of any of the unpublished, confidential Exhibit B works at the February 21, 1995 hearing, the court indicated that its Amended TRO would "prohibit any publication of confidential matter or any publication of copyrighted matter that was not that which is fair criticism or comment or fair use." Erlich's March 15, 1995 Opp'n, Ex. A, Tr. 30-31. Erlich may have reasonably misconstrued this language so that he believed the exception for fair use also modified the first clause, "prohibit[ing] any publication of confidential matter," especially given Erlich's *pro se* status at the hearing. Accordingly, the court does not find that plaintiffs have shown by clear and convincing evidence that Erlich's mistake was not a "good faith and reasonable interpretation of the [court's oral] order." *In re Dual-Deck Video Cassette Antitrust Litigation,*https://apps.fastcase.com/Research/Pages/Document.aspx?LTID=v%2b%2bWn0p FJOPwVn7bDpURwR5rY%2bXX9Uta8hAwg5stZDj8s EobQkSQ %2bky70Tw1SszD6GuoylZ859kfbr0CHnkdXRmwxL W7cJtCJym 88GmTgsrrExWnNNSNiN61CAkvo365&ECF=10+F.3d +at+695 10 F.3dat 695. Although the court is not convinced that Erlich's use of the Exhibit B works, to which the fair use defense would not have applied at the time, was in any case a fair use, the defense was not adequately explained in the context of the hearing such that Erlich's violation could be considered a violation of a "specific and definite" court order. *See id.*

B. Second Alleged Contempt

Plaintiffs allege that Erlich provided copies of one of Hubbard's Advanced Technology writings to another litigant to be used in a declaration. As the court found in its May 5, 1995 "Order Denying Plaintiffs' Ex Parte Application To Shorten Time re Contempt Hearing," plaintiffs have not demonstrated how Erlich has clearly violated the Amended TRO, which prohibited certain uses of the Exhibits to the complaint, by attaching to a declaration a work not listed in the Exhibits to the complaint but merely "related to" one of those works. Plaintiffs have submitted no new evidence on this issue that would lead the court to change its earlier ruling.

C. Third Alleged Contempt

Third, plaintiffs allege that on May 15, 1995, an interview of Erlich appeared on a BBC television show which contained a segment related to this case. Plaintiffs have attached a declaration stating that plaintiffs believe Erlich disclosed information "taken right out of" one part of the Advanced Technology listed in Exhibit B-1[34] to the First Amended Complaint. Erlich disputes that he disclosed any portion of the Exhibit B works on the British television show, and argues that the information he disclosed is already widely available to the public, as evidenced by several articles in newspapers and magazines. Erlich further objects to the declaration of Warren McShane offered by plaintiffs, as it lacks foundation for the content of the BBC interview. Even accepting the validity of McShane's declaration regarding what was disclosed on the BBC show, the court finds that plaintiffs have failed to prove by clear and convincing evidence that Erlich in fact disclosed any of the Exhibit B works which were the subject of the Amended TRO. To the extent that Erlich's extremely brief statement relating to the Advanced Technology discloses information from one of those works, the court further finds that Erlich stated nothing more than has appeared in numerous newspaper and magazine articles and books about the Church. *See, e.g.,* Joel Sappell & Robert W. Welkos, "The Man Behind the Religion" *L.A. Times,* June 24, 1990, at A36, Oakley May 31, 1995 Decl., Ex. C, at 81.

V. ERLICH'S MOTION TO VACATE WRIT OF SEIZURE

Erlich challenges the February 10, 1995 writ of seizure[35] on the grounds that it was

Page 1261

not authorized under the Federal Rules and that it is unconstitutionally overbroad. Erlich seeks the vacation of the writ of seizure, the return of all materials seized, and an increase in the amount of the bond.

Erlich argues that the writ of seizure is invalid because plaintiffs did not comply with the requirements of Rule 65(b) of the Federal Rules of Civil Procedure. Plaintiffs respond that the seizure was authorized by the Supreme Court's Copyright Rules, which provide for a summary process of seizure separate from the Federal Rules. Plaintiffs further argue that, even if Rule 65(b) applies, its requirements were met prior to the issuance of the writ.

A. Supreme Court's Copyright Rules

The 1976 Act provides for the impoundment of allegedly infringing articles:

At any time while an action under this title is pending, the court *may* order the impounding, on such terms as it deems reasonable, of all copies ... claimed to have been made or used in violation of the copyright owner's exclusive rights, and of all plates, molds, matrices, masters, tapes, film negatives, or other articles by means of which such copies ... may be reproduced.

17 U.S.C. § 503(a) (emphasis added). Unlike the 1909 Act, the 1976 Act gives the court discretion whether to issue an impounding order. 3 Nimmer § 14.07, at 14-112.

In 1909, the Supreme Court issued Copyright Rules ("Rules"), pursuant to section 25(e) of the 1909 Act, setting forth procedures for seizure and impoundment. *See* 17 U.S.C. foll. § 501. The Rules allow the clerk of the court to summarily issue a writ of seizure of allegedly infringing articles without requiring any preseizure notice or hearing.

Paramount Pictures Corp. v. Doe, 821 F.Supp. 82, 86

(E.D.N.Y.1993); 3 Nimmer § 14.07, at 14-113 to -114. Although neither the Supreme Court nor the 1976 Act explicitly repealed the Copyright Rules, *Warner Bros. Inc. v. Dae Rim Trading, Inc.,* 877 F.2d 1120, 1124 (2d Cir.1989), courts and commentators have questioned the Rules' continuing validity, both as a matter of statutory construction and constitutional law. *See WPOW, Inc. v. MRLJ Enterprises,* 584 F.Supp. 132, 134-35 (D.D.C.1984)

(rejecting continuing validity of Rules based on added discretion in 1976 Act which is inconsistent with summary and mandatory procedure of Rules); *Paramount,*https://apps.fastcase.com

/Research/Pages/Document.aspx?LTID=v%2b%2b
Wn0pFJOPwV
n7bDpURwR5rY%2bXX9Uta8hAwg5stZDj8sEobQkS
Q%2bky70
Tw1SszD6GuoylZ859kfbr0CHnkdXRmwxLW7cJtCJy
m88GmTgs
rrExWnNNSNiN61CAkvo365&ECF=821+F.Supp.+at+
87-91 821

F.Supp. at 87-91 & n. 4 (finding provisions of Rules "clearly inconsistent with the discretionary powers" of the 1976 Act, noting that the 1976 Act "arguably supersedes and renders null and void" the Rules, and holding that Rules run afoul of Fourth and Fifth Amendments); *Van Deurzen & Assoc. v. Sanders,* 21 U.S.P.Q.2d 1480, 1991 WL 183817 (D.Kan.1991); 3 Nimmer § 14.07, at 14-

115 to -119 (noting that Rules' ex parte proceedings are subject to "serious question" as to whether they violate free speech, due process, and freedom from unreasonable searches and seizures); *cf. First Technology Safety Systems, Inc. v. Depinet,* 11 F.3d 641, 648- 49 & n. 8 (6th Cir.1993) (noting debate regarding sufficiency of compliance with Rules and applying Fed.R.Civ.P. 65(b) where seizure not authorized by Rules).

Plaintiffs cite *Duchess Music Corp. v. Stern,* 458 F.2d 1305 (9th Cir.), *cert. denied sub nom. Rosner v. Duchess Music Corp.,* 409 U.S. 847, 93 S.Ct. 52, 34 L.Ed.2d 88 (1972) to support their position that the Rules still permit a summary procedure for the ex parte granting of writs of seizure. In *Duchess,* the Ninth Circuit reversed the district

Page 1262

court's order that certain seized items be returned, holding that "[n]either the [1909 Act] nor the Supreme Court rules give the District Court any discretion to determine what to impound" and that the "process Congress granted the aggrieved copyright proprietor is a summary one." *Id.* at 1308. Given the discretionary language of the 1976 Act, and the expansion of the Fifth Amendment in cases such as *Mitchell v. W.T. Grant Co.,* 416 U.S. 600, 94 S.Ct. 1895, 40 L.Ed.2d 406 (1974), the court finds plaintiffs' reliance on the Copyright Rules and *Duchess* to be misplaced. Instead, the court finds persuasive the reasoning of the courts in *Paramount* and *WPOW* questioning the current validity of the summary process approved by the 1909 Act and Supreme Court Rules and requiring plaintiffs to meet the requirements of Rule 65(b) of the Federal Rules of Civil Procedure.

B. Requirements of Rule 65(b)

Rule 65(b) provides that ex parte injunctive relief will be granted only if (1) it clearly appears from specific facts shown by affidavit or by the verified complaint that *immediate and irreparable injury,* loss, or damage will result to the applicant before the adverse party or that party's attorney can be heard in opposition, and (2) the applicant's attorney certifies to the court in writing the ... *reasons supporting the claim that notice should not be required.*

Fed.R.Civ.P. 65(b) (emphasis added).

i. Irreparable Injury

In their ex parte applications for relief, plaintiffs argued that interim injunctive relief was necessary because Erlich had repeatedly infringed plaintiffs' copyrighted works, even after being warned by plaintiffs. In his deposition, McShane testified that plaintiffs would suffer injury from Erlich's unauthorized posting of plaintiffs' works because "if people read those documents they're not supposed to, and if that affects them from ever doing the service, stops them from doing the service, obviously they won't make donations to the church which will directly affect RTC economically." Oakley Reply Decl., Ex. B, at 112. McShane also stated that he was "quite concerned that [Erlich] will continue to defy requests to cease infringement even if ordered to do so by the Court. Mr. Erlich has already placed multiple copyrighted works, including several that are confidential, onto a massive computer network potentially accessed by 25 million people." McShane February 8, 1995 Decl. ¶

56. The court finds this evidence sufficient to establish a likelihood that, absent a writ of seizure,

Erlich would have continued to post plaintiffs' copyrighted works prior to a hearing. Such a likelihood of further infringement before Erlich could respond, combined with a reasonable likelihood of success on the copyright infringement claim, allows the court to presume irreparable injury. *See Apple,*https://apps.fastcase.com/Research/Pages/Document.aspx?L TID=v%2b%2bWn0pFJOPwVn7bDpURwR5rY%2bXX 9Uta8hA wg5stZDj8sEobQkSQ%2bky70Tw1SszD6GuoylZ859kf br0CHnkd XRmwxLW7cJtCJym88GmTgsrrExWnNNSNiN61CA kvo365&E CF=725+F.2d+at+525 725 F.2d at 525 (holding that reasonable likelihood of success of copyright infringement claim allows presumption of irreparable injury);

*WPOW,*https://apps.fastcase.com/Research/Pages/Document.aspx?LTID=v%2b%2bWn0pFJOPwVn7bDpURwR5rY%2bX X9Uta8h Awg5stZDj8sEobQkSQ%2bky70Tw1SszD6GuoylZ859 kfbr0CHn kdXRmwxLW7cJtCJym88GmTgsrrExWnNNSNiN61CAkvo365& ECF=584+F.Supp.+at+138 584 F.Supp. at 138 (allowing presumption in context of impoundment).

3. Reasons Why Notice Should Not Be Required

The second element of Rule 65(b) permits injunctive relief without notice only where notice to the adverse party is impossible or, in some limited circumstances, where notice would render further action fruitless. *First Technology,*https://apps.fastcase.com/Research/Pages/Document.aspx?LTID=v%2b%2bWn0pFJOPwVn7bDpURwR5rY%2bXX9Uta8hAwg5stZDj8sEobQkSQ%2bky70Tw1SszD6GuoylZ859kfbr0CHnkdXRmwxLW7cJtCJym88GmTgsrrExWnNNSNiN61CAkvo365&ECF=11+F.3d+at+650 11 F.3d at

650. Plaintiffs may meet the latter exception to the notice requirement by showing that Erlich "would have disregarded a direct court order and disposed of the goods within the time it would take for a hearing."

Id.; 3 Nimmer § 14.07, at 14-115. This may be shown with evidence of a defendant's history of violating court orders or destroying evidence, such as in the case of a member of a counterfeiting ring who, if given notice, would simply transfer his inventories to another member of the ring.[36] *Id.; In re Vuitton et Fils S.A.*, 606

Page 1263

F.2d 1, 4-5 (2d Cir.1979). Plaintiffs provide evidence of the need for a pre- notice seizure: Erlich stated that the decision whether to stop posting Scientology works was his and that "[n]o local government or court in the [U.S.] has the power to tell [him] otherwise." FAC, Ex. J. Although the court was persuaded at the time of its seizure order that this evidence indicated that there was a chance that Erlich would not follow a court order, the court has reconsidered its original conclusion. Erlich's statement of defiance, made in the context of an exchange of hostile letters between the parties, does not rise to the level necessary to meet Rule 65(b)'s demanding requirements for dispensing with notice. Further, other than this isolated statement, there was no evidence of Erlich's propensity to defy a court order. The court does not find that this case is analogous to that of a counterfeiter who, if given notice, might transfer the infringing works elsewhere. Erlich is not "engaged primarily in illegitimate and infringing activities and [is thus not] likely to disregard an order from [the court] preventing [him] from disposing of or destroying any [evidence of infringement]." *Paramount,* https://apps.fastcase.com/Research/Pages/Document.aspx?LTID=v

%2b%2bWn0pFJOPwVn7bDpURwR5rY%2bXX9Uta8hAwg5stZ Dj8sEobQkSQ%2bky70Tw1SszD6GuoylZ859kfbr0CHnkdXRmw xLW7cJtCJym88GmTgsrrExWnNNSNiN61CAkvo365&ECF=82 1+F.Supp.+at+89 821 F.Supp. at 89. The court further notes that plaintiffs already had evidence of Erlich's infringing copies in the form of the newsgroup postings, thereby reducing the importance of preserving other evidence of infringement.

Because there was an insufficient showing under Rule 65(b) to support a writ of seizure, the writ must be vacated.[37]

C. Unconstitutionally Overbroad?

Although the court has found that the requirements of Rule 65(b) were not sufficiently met, the court further notes that one aspect of the order was overbroad. "It is well settled that the Fourth Amendment prohibition against unreasonable intrusions ... governs not only criminal investigations but also searches and seizures made pursuant to civil proceedings," *Paramount,*https://apps.fastcase.com

/Research/Pages/Document.aspx?LTID=v%2b%2bWn0pFJOPwV n7bDpURwR5rY%2bXX9Uta8hAwg5stZDj8sEobQkSQ%2bky70 Tw1SszD6GuoylZ859kfbr0CHnkdXRmwxLW7cJtCJy m88GmTgs rrExWnNNSNiN61CAkvo365&ECF=821+F.Supp.+at+90 821

F.Supp. at 90 (citing *Soldal v. Cook County, Ill.*, 506 U.S. 56, 66-67 & n.10, 113 S.Ct. 538, 546 & n. 10, 121 L.Ed.2d 450 (1992)),

including "seizure orders directing the United States Marshal to impound allegedly infringing articles under the Copyright Act," *id.* (citing *Warner Bros., Inc. v. Dae Rim Trading, Inc.*, 677 F.Supp. 740, 765 (S.D.N.Y. 1988), *aff'd in part, rev'd in part on other grounds*,https://apps.fastcase.com/Research/Pages/Document.aspx

?LTID=v

%2b%2bWn0pFJOPwVn7bDpURwR5rY%2bXX9 Uta8hAwg5stZ Dj8sEobQkSQ%2bky70Tw1SszD6GuoylZ859kfbr0CH nkdXRmw xLW7cJtCJym88GmTgsrrExWnNNSNiN61CAkvo365 &ECF=87 7+F.2d+1120+%282d+Cir.1989%29 877 F.2d 1120 (2dCir.1989)).

To comply with the requirements of the Fourth Amendment, a writ of seizure should specify with particularity the premises to be searched and the articles to be seized. *Id.* The scope of the search must thus be limited by "the object of the search and the places in which there has been a showing that the object is likely to be found." *Id.* (citing *Maryland v. Garrison,* 480 U.S. 79, 84, 107 S.Ct.

1013, 1016, 94 L.Ed.2d 72 (1987)). The order should "enable the executing officer to ascertain and identify with reasonable certainty those items that the [court] has authorized him to seize." *Time Warner Entertainment Co. v. Does,* 876 F.Supp. 407, 413 (E.D.N.Y.1994) (citing *United States v.George,* 975 F.2d 72, 75 (2d Cir.1992)).

The purpose of preliminary injunctive relief is to maintain the status quo. Impoundment is also meant to allow for a possible remedy of destruction of the infringing articles. 3 Nimmer § 14.07, at 14-119. To the extent that the order allowed the seizure of "articles and things that appear to be works of L. Ron Hubbard protected by copyrights," it went beyond the purpose of the Copyright Act to prevent the unauthorized "reproduction" of protected works; the mere possession of copyrighted works does not offend the Copyright Act. This language is also somewhat vague, as it describes a category of works which cannot be identified by any easy to apply criteria. The criteria used to determine what items are to be seized

Page 1264

must not be overly subjective, such that the decision of what to seize rests solely in the hands of plaintiffs' expert rather than the U.S. Marshal.

*Paramount,*https://apps.fastcase.com/Research/Pages/Document.as px?LTID=v%2b%2bWn0pFJOPwVn7bDpURwR5rY% 2bXX9Uta 8hAwg5stZDj8sEobQkSQ%2bky70Tw1SszD6GuoylZ8 59kfbr0C HnkdXRmwxLW7cJtCJym88GmTgsrrExWnNNSNiN 61CAkvo36 5&ECF=821+F.Supp.+at+91 821 F.Supp. at 91 (finding application constitutionally deficient where only some of distinguishing markings for identifying unauthorized video- cassettes were listed in plaintiffs' application); *Time Warner,*https://apps.fastcase.com

/Research/Pages/Document.aspx?LTID=v%2b%2b Wn0pFJOPwV n7bDpURwR5rY%2bXX9Uta8hAwg5stZDj8sEobQkS

Q%2bky70
Tw1SszD6GuoylZ859kfbr0CHnkdXRmwxLW7cJtCJy
m88GmTgs
rrExWnNNSNiN61CAkvo365&ECF=876+F.Supp.+at+
413 876

F.Supp. at 413 (finding plaintiffs' application insufficient where murky photocopies of copyrighted designs and trademarks provided insufficient guidance to marshal). Here, there were no specific criteria given by which a marshal could identify which works were written by Hubbard and were protected by copyrights. In effect, this language gave plaintiffs' experts the authority to search through Erlich's possessions and computer files using their discretion in deciding what to seize, unchecked by any law enforcement officials.

Plaintiffs contend, however, that its use of a computer expert to enable the search of materials on Erlich's computers and an expert in the works of Scientology to enable the identification of plaintiffs' works was justified, citing a criminal case, *State v. Wade,* 544 So.2d 1028, 1030-31 (Fla.Dist.Ct. App.1989). In *Wade,* the Florida appellate court upheld a search for stolen computer equipment where law enforcement officers were aided by computer consultants employed by the victim computer manufacturer. *Id.* The *Wade* court reasoned that searches in areas beyond law enforcement officers' expertise necessitate the use of experts and noted that the employees of the victim are perhaps the best experts to identify the allegedly stolen equipment. *Id.* at 1030 (citing 2 Wayne R. LaFave, *Search & Seizure* § 4.11(b), at 343 (1987) (commenting that practice of using victims to help advise in search is unobjectionable in exceptional situations such as where only the victim can adequately identify what items are stolen)).[38] The court finds that, in the context of identification of allegedly infringing copies of literary works, use of an expert to *aid* the marshal may be justified. In this case, the number of potentially infringed works was too great to permit the plaintiffs to bring originals to be used in verifying the source of copies. Accordingly, plaintiffs were justified in using an expert to identify the allegedly infringing works. Similarly, because the allegedly infringing copies were likely to be stored on a computer, the use of computer experts was justified to aid in finding the materials.[39] *See*

*Wade,*https://apps.fastcase.com/Research/Pages/Document.aspx?LTID=v%2b%2bWn0pFJOPwVn7bDpURwR5rY%2bXX9Uta8hAwg5stZDj8sEobQkSQ%2bky70Tw1SszD6GuoylZ859kfbr0CHnkdXRmwxLW7cJtCJym88GmTgsrrExWnNNSNiN61CAkvo365&E CF=544+So.2d+at+1030 544 So.2d at 1030; *cf.* Oakley Reply Decl., Ex. C, at 200 (Erlich Depo.) (indicating that police officers at seizure were not computer literate).

However, such works should have been adequately identified before the seizure to "ensure[] that the search [would] be carefully tailored to its justifications and [would] not take on the character of the wide- ranging exploratory searches the Framers intended to prohibit." *Paramount,*https://apps.fastcase.com/Research/Pages/Document.aspx?LTID=v%2b%2bWn0pFJOPwVn7bDpURwR5rY%2bXX9Uta

8hAwg5stZDj8sEobQkSQ%2bky70Tw1SszD6GuoylZ8 59kfbr0C

HnkdXRmwxLW7cJtCJym88GmTgsrrExWnNNSNiN 61CAkvo36 5&ECF=821+F.Supp.+at+90 821 F.Supp. at 90 (quoting *Garrison,*https://apps.fastcase.com/Research/Pages/Document.aspx

?LTID=v%2b%2bWn0pFJOPwVn7bDpURwR5rY %2bXX9Uta8h Awg5stZDj8sEobQkSQ%2bky70Tw1SszD6GuoylZ859 kfbr0CHn kdXRmwxLW7cJtCJym88GmTgsrrExWnNNSNiN61C Akvo365& ECF=480+U.S.+at+84 480 U.S. at 84, 107 S.Ct. at 1016). The inclusion of language allowing the seizure of "any articles and things appearing to be works of L. Ron Hubbard protected by copyrights" arguably made the writ overbroad, giving RTC officials too much discretion in identifying Hubbard works and in determining which works were subject to copyright protection and which copies were unauthorized. In effect, plaintiffs' agents were given the authority to seize even lawfully owned copies of Hubbard's works for which there was no evidence of any infringing use, which exceeds the authority of 17 U.S.C. § 503(a).

Page 1265

D. Conclusion

Because plaintiffs' ex parte application for a writ of seizure did not meet the requirements of Rule 65(b), the court vacates the writ. Plaintiffs must return to Erlich all articles seized within ten (10) days of this order.[40]

VI. PLAINTIFFS' REQUEST FOR SANCTIONS AGAINST CARLA OAKLEY

The court is disturbed by the parties' seemingly endless applications to the court, consolidated oppositions, sur-replies, objections to sur- replies, and other such inappropriate pleadings. In their objections to Erlich's "Consolidated Opposition to Plaintiffs' Ex Parte Applications," plaintiffs request that Erlich's counsel, Ms. Carla Oakley, be sanctioned under Rule 11 of the Federal Rules of Civil Procedure and 28 U.S.C. § 1927 for filing "frivolous" pleadings which multiply the proceedings "unreasonably and vexatiously."

To the extent that the Consolidated Opposition contains new arguments, the court finds that these arguments are necessary to address plaintiffs' multiple ex parte applications alleging three different instances of contempt. Erlich's sur-reply to the motion to expand the TRO was arguably justified by plaintiffs' mention of a new instance of alleged contempt for the first time in their Reply.[41] The court therefore denies plaintiffs' requests for sanctions. Plaintiffs' request that the court strike the arguments in the Consolidated Opposition because they are merely repetitive arguments that were "cut and past[ed]" from previous briefs is unnecessary to the extent that the briefs add nothing new. However, the court orders that the parties not file any further post-Reply briefing, which only wastes the court's and parties' resources, without first seeking leave of the court. *See* Civil L.R. 7- 3(e). The court further rejects plaintiffs' claim that Erlich's "Consolidated Opposition" reveals alleged trade secrets from plaintiffs' Advanced Technology works, and should have been filed under seal. Nothing in the "Consolidated Opposition" reveals information not already publicized in the popular press. *See supra* part IV.C.

VII. ORDER

For the reasons set forth above, the court orders as follows:

1. Defendant Dennis Erlich and his agents, servants, and employees, all persons acting or purporting to act under his authority, direction or control, and all persons acting in concert or in participation with any of them who receive notice of this Order, shall be and are restrained and enjoined pending further court order:

   a. From all unauthorized reproduction, transmission, and publication of any of the works of L. Ron Hubbard that are protected under the Copyright Act of 1976, as codified in its amended form at 17 U.S.C. § 101 et seq. Such works are found, for the purposes of this order only, to be those works identified in Exhibits A and B to the complaint, except for item 4 of Exhibit A. A copy of said exhibits are attached hereto with item 4 of Exhibit A redacted.

b. Unauthorized reproduction, transmission, or publication includes placement of a copyrighted work into a computer's hard drive or other storage device; "browsing" the text of a copyrighted work resident on another computer through on- screen examination; scanning a copyrighted work into a digital file; "uploading" a digital file containing a copyrighted work from the computer to a bulletin board system or other server; "downloading" a digital file containing a copyrighted work from a bulletin board system or other server to the computer; and "quoting" a copyrighted work that is cited in an on-line message in sending, responding to or forwarding that message.

c. Nothing in this section of the order shall be construed to prohibit fair use of such works, as set forth in 17 U.S.C. § 107 and interpreted by applicable case law. Fair use of the copyrighted material for the purposes of this order includes use of the copyrighted work for

> the purpose of criticism, news reporting, teaching, scholarship, and research but does not include: use of the material for a commercial purpose where the user stands to profit from exploitation of the copyrighted material without paying the customary price or giving the usual consideration or use that would have a significant effect on the potential market value of the copyrighted work; (2) use which fulfills the demand for the original work; or (3) use of the heart of the work — no more of a work may be taken than is necessary to make any accompanying comment understandable. With respect to unpublished materials, the amount of copied material must comprise only a very small percentage of the copyrighted works both from a quantitative and a qualitative standpoint.

The prior postings by defendant Erlich that form the basis of this order do not qualify as fair use primarily because of the quantity of the material posted and the very limited transformative use made of those materials. Identical or similar postings are therefore enjoined.

d. From destroying, altering, concealing or removing from the district in which defendant Erlich resides, any reproduction, copy, facsimile, excerpt or derivative of any work of L. Ron Hubbard that is described in Exhibit A or B including all such works returned pursuant to this order.

Defendant Erlich or his counsel shall safely retain possession of any such items.

e. A condition of this preliminary injunction is that a $25,000 bond shall be posted (or continued in place) pursuant to Federal Rule of Civil Procedure 65(c).
f. Plaintiffs' application to expand the TRO is denied without prejudice.
g. Plaintiffs' motion for a finding of contempt against defendant Erlich is denied.
h. Plaintiffs are ordered to return within ten (10) days of the date of this order to defendant Erlich through his counsel all items seized

pursuant to the writ of seizure issued February 10, 1995.

i. Plaintiffs' request for sanctions against defendant Erlich's counsel, Ms. Carla Oakley, is denied.

Notes:

1. The Internet is a world-wide network of networks, made up of approximately 7 million computers interconnected through 60,000 networks, all sharing a common communications technology. Anthony M. Rutkowski, *Federal News Service,* July 27, 1995. It is decentralized in that there is no central hub through which information must be routed and no central governing body. *United States v. Baker,* 890 F.Supp. 1375 at 1379 n. 1 (E.D.Mich.1995). Started as a project by the Department of Defense, the Internet has expanded to include universities, government agencies, and commercial enterprises. There are currently over 25 million users worldwide accessing the Internet, and the numbers are doubling every year. *MTV Networks v. Curry,* 867 F.Supp. 202, 203 n. 1 (S.D.N.Y.1994).

Users of the Internet can access such services as e-mail, Usenet newsgroups, file exchanges, and the "World Wide Web," a distributed hypertext information service, accessed using a "Web browser." *Guardian,* Sept. 1, 1994, at T8.

2. Plaintiffs additionally sued defendants Tom Klemesrud ("Klemesrud"), who operates the bulletin board service ("BBS") used by Erlich, and Netcom On-Line Communication Services, Inc. ("Netcom"), who provides that BBS with access to the Internet.
3. The court will address plaintiffs' motion for a preliminary injunction against Klemesrud and Netcom, Klemesrud's motion for judgment on the pleadings, and Netcom's motion for summary judgment in a separate order.
4. Plaintiffs describe the works of the "Scientology Religion" as "applied religious philosophy and spiritual healing technology." First Am. Compl. ("FAC") ¶ 9. The Ninth Circuit described the Church's teachings as follows:

The Church ... teaches that a person's behavior and well-being are improved by removing "engrams" from the unconscious mind. Engrams are impressions recorded by the unconscious mind in times of trauma in this life or in previous lives. Engrams return in moments of similar stress to the detriment of the person's behavior. Removing engrams from the unconscious permits the person's analytical mind to function unhindered.

Engrams are located and purged through "auditing." Auditing uses the "technology" and "advanced technology" of the Church The adherent must proceed through a series of increasingly sophisticated technologies of closely structured questions and answers to reach "a higher spiritual existence."

The Church asserts that the unsupervised, premature exposure of an adherent to these materials will produce a spiritually harmful effect.

Religious

(9th Cir.1986), *cert.*

Center v. Wollersheim, 796 F.2d 1076, 1077 *denied,*https://apps.fastcase.com/Research/Pages/Document.as

px?LTID=v%2b%2bWn0pFJOPwVn7bDpURwR5rY%2bXX 9Uta8hAwg5stZDj8sEobQkSQ%2bky70Tw1SszD6GuoylZ85 9kfbr0CHnkdXRmwxLW7cJtCJym88GmTgsrrExWnNNSNi N61CAkvo365&ECF=479+U.S.+1103 479 U.S. 1103, 107 S.Ct. 1336, 94 L.Ed.2d 187 (1987).

5. Usenet news, which is one of the most popular features of the Internet, allows users of systems "subscribing" to the groups to participate by reading and "posting" messages on a particular topic, such as intellectual property rights ("misc. int-property") or table tennis ("rec.sport.table-tennis"). "Posting," as a noun, refers to an article in a newsgroup and, as a verb, refers to the act of sending an article one has written for distribution to the newsgroup's subscribers. When a message is posted to a group, it is distributed to the computers of all those systems that subscribe to that group so that the users of that system can access the message. There are currently thousands of different newsgroups,

with about 50,000 new articles posted each day. John R. Levine & Carol Baroudi, *The Internet for Dummies* 131 (2d ed. 1994).

6. Erlich gained access to the Internet by using a personal computer and a modem in his home to connect to defendant Klemesrud's BBS, to which Erlich was one of 512 subscribers paying an annual fee. Klemesrud Decl. 13. Klemesrud's BBS, in turn, was connected to the Internet through an arrangement with defendant Netcom under which Klemesrud leased access to the Internet at a fixed rate.
7. These works are part of the "course" materials used in the upper- levels of Scientology training, and are only available to those Scientologists who have successfully completed all of the lower courses.
8. The parties treated the motion to dissolve the TRO as superseding the earlier application for a preliminary injunction. The court finds no differences in the legal standards for dissolving a TRO and for granting a preliminary injunction, except for the potentially different relevant time-frames. Here, both motions concern whether

further injunctive relief prior to trial is appropriate. Accordingly, the motions will be discussed together.

9. Although the court concludes in its discussion of the trade secrets claim, *infra* part II.C.3, that most of the Exhibit B works may no longer contain trade secrets (assuming they ever did), this does not mean that, for the purposes of copyright protection, they are not unpublished. "Publication," as defined in 17 U.S.C. § 101, requires that the owner *consent* to selling, leasing, loaning, giving away, or otherwise making available to the general public, the original or copies of the work. 1 Nimmer § 4.04, at 4-17 to -19 & n. 8. There is no evidence of any consensual release of any of these works to the public.
10. The court is unpersuaded by the various alleged technical deficiencies, such as title discrepancies, in the copyright registrations. Errors, such as incorrectly naming the author, do not make the copyright invalid absent some evidence that the defendant was misled. 2 Nimmer § 7.20, at 7-201 to-207.

11. The court will address the issue of direct infringement more fully in its order on the motions concerning defendants Netcom and Klemesrud.
12. Even though fair use is an affirmative defense, *Harper & Row, Publishers, Inc. v. Nation Enterprises,* 471 U.S. 539, 561, 105 S.Ct. 2218, 2231, 85 L.Ed.2d 588 (1985), the court notes that plaintiffs, as the parties moving for a preliminary injunction, have the burden of proving a likelihood of success on their infringement claim, including the fair use defense. *See* 2 William Schwarzer et al., *California Practice Guide: Federal Civil Procedure Before Trial* ¶ 13:47 (1994) (citing *Original Appalachian Artworks v. Topps Chewing Gum,* 642 F.Supp. 1031, 1034 (N.D.Ga. 1986)). However, in determining whether plaintiffs have met their burden, the court recognizes that fair use is an affirmative defense on which defendants will have the burden of proof at trial.
13. Erlich responds that the documents that he posted "speak for themselves," and thus little further commentary was necessary. The court

will address this dispute under the third statutory factor.

14. Plaintiffs cite *Sega Enterprises Ltd. v. Maphia,* 857 F.Supp. 679 (N.D.Cal.1994) for the proposition that there can be no fair use defense where the defendant did not use an authorized copy to make his copies. In *Sega,* the defendant, who had allegedly copied Sega videogame cartridges onto an electronic BBS where others could copy them, *id.* at 683, admitted that he did not own any copies of Sega's game cartridges, *id.* at 687. *Sega* relies on language from *Atari Games Corp. v. Nintendo of America Inc.,* 975 F.2d 832, 843 (Fed.Cir.1992) stating that "[t]o invoke the fair use exception, an individual must possess an authorized copy of a literary work." *Atari,* in turn, relies on *Harper & Row's* discussion of the first statutory factor. In *Harper & Row,*https://apps.fastcase.com/Research/Pages

/Document.aspx?LTID=v%2b%2bWn0pFJOPwVn
7bDpURw
R5rY%2bXX9Uta8hAwg5stZDj8sEobQkSQ%2bky70T
w1Ssz

D6GuoylZ859kfbr0CHnkdXRmwxLW7cJtCJym88Gm TgsrrE xWnNNSNiN61CAkvo365&ECF=471+U.S.+at+563 471 U.S.

at 563, 105 S.Ct. at 2232, the Supreme Court cited the trial court's finding that the defendant "knowingly exploited a purloined manuscript" as weighing against a finding of fair use on the first factor. Nothing in *Harper & Row* indicates that the defendant's bad faith was itself conclusive of the fair use question, or even of the first factor. After *Campbell,* it is clear that a finding of bad faith, or a finding on any one of the four factors, cannot be considered dispositive.

*Campbell,*https://apps.fastcase.com/Research/Pages /Document

.aspx?LTID=v%2b%2bWn0pFJOPwVn7bDpURw R5rY%2bX X9Uta8hAwg5stZDj8sEobQkSQ%2bky70Tw1SszD6G uoylZ8 59kfbr0CHnkdXRmwxLW7cJtCJym88GmTgsrrExWn NNSNi N61CAkvo365&ECF=510+U.S.+at+ %2c+ 510 U.S. at

-, & n. 18, 114 S.Ct. at 1170-71, 1174 & n. 18.

Campbell cited *Harper & Row's* good faith discussion without comment, but noted that the defendant's use of the plaintiff's work, despite the plaintiff's explicit denial of permission, would not, in any case, constitute bad faith. *Id.* at_n. 18, 114 S.Ct. at 1174 n. 18. *Campbell,* the Supreme Court's most recent pronouncement on fair use, thus hardly endorses the good faith requirement. *See* 3 Nimmer § 13.05[B][3], at 13- 205 n. 298. Accordingly, the court will treat bad faith as merely one aspect of the first factor.

15. The court is unpersuaded by plaintiffs' argument that an intermediate copy made for the purposes of posting or uploading a work makes the subsequent copy unauthorized such that fair use is unavailable. *Sega* and

Atari merely suggest that fair use is unavailable where the defendant does not possess *any authorized copy;* not that the challenged copying cannot be made from a secondary copy. While the extra copying may constitute infringement (for which there may or may not be a separate fair use defense), it should not affect the availability of the fair use defense as to the critical or parodic use.

16. Somewhat inconsistently, Erlich argues on the trade secret claim that many of the Exhibit B works are "more prosaic than formulaic." Reply at 13.
17. Erlich also argues that, even if he did copy most or all of many of the works, he copied no more than was reasonable for his purposes. Erlich cites *Belmore v. City Pages, Inc.*, 880 F.Supp. 673, 678-79 (D.Minn.1995), in which the court found fair use where the defendant copied verbatim an entire short article from a police newspaper for the purpose of criticism with added commentary constituting only about one fourth of the defendant's article. The court found reasonable the alleged infringer's explanation that he copied the original in its entirety because the original "took the form of a parable and was relatively short" and because he "decided that the repulsive message it appeared to convey could not be adequately communicated except by printing the story as a whole." *Id.* at 679. Erlich fails to

mention that the *Belmore* court concluded that the third factor weighed in favor of the plaintiff; only a strong showing by the defendant on the first and fourth factor overcame the fact that the defendant had copied the entire work. Moreover, unlike the defendant in *Belmore,* Erlich never adequately explains why it was essential for him to copy verbatim the amount of the works that he copied, merely asserting in a conclusory fashion that it was "reasonable in relation to the purpose of the copying." Further, Erlich's added criticism was far less substantial than the thirty-four lines of added commentary in *Belmore.* The court is unconvinced that Erlich's wholesale copying of Hubbard's works with little or no commentary was necessary for his critical purposes.

18. To the extent that courts look at how much of the allegedly *infringing work* is made up of copied material, *see Harper &*

*Row,*https://apps.fastcase.com/Research/Pages/Document.aspx

?LTID=v%2b%2bWn0pFJOPwVn7bDpURwR5rY %2bXX9U

ta8hAwg5stZDj8sEobQkSQ%2bky70Tw1SszD6G uoylZ859kf br0CHnkdXRmwxLW7cJtCJym88GmTgsrrExWnNNS NiN61 CAkvo365&ECF=471+U.S.+at+565-66 471 U.S. at 565-66,

105 S.Ct. at 2233, this factor also weighs heavily against Erlich.

Most of Erlich's postings constitute verbatim quotes from Hubbard's works, with occasional commentary such as "The perfect reference for any occasion," "I believe a discussion of this policy is in order," "Any questions?" and "Someone requested this, I assume, to discuss." Standing alone, these remarks are hardly criticism or commentary.

However, Erlich argues that the critical nature of Erlich's postings must be viewed in light of the extended nature of "threads" on newsgroups. A thread is an article on a particular topic, together with all the follow-up articles, and the follow- ups to the follow-ups. Levine & Baroudi, *supra* note 5, at 399. While an entire thread might be considered one composite work authored by all those adding to the thread, there is no evidence in the record that any of Erlich's postings were followed up with further comments or criticism on the works that are excerpted. Erlich argues that it is common practice on the Internet to repeat large portions of a previous posting verbatim, which is necessary to add context for those who are late in joining a discussion. While this would perhaps justify the copying of works that were previously posted by their authors on the basis of an implied license or fair use argument, *see* Maureen A. O'Rourke, "The Future of Copyright and Contract Law in a Networked World," *Federal Bar News & Journal* (August 1994), these defenses would not apply where the first posting made an unauthorized copy of a copyrighted work. The court accepts, however, the possibility that a particular quotation of a copyrighted work in the context of a long thread that involves significant criticism or commentary could be fair use.

19. To the extent that Erlich's postings suppress demand for the original works by "persuad[ing] [potential buyers] that Hubbard was a charlatan"

or that the Church is a fraud, as clearly Erlich intends, such a "devastating critique" is not "within the scope of copyright protection." *New Era,*https://apps.fastcase.com/ Research/Pages/Document.aspx?LTID=v%2b

%2bWn0pFJOPwVn7bDpURwR5rY%2bXX9Uta8 hAwg5stZ Dj8sEobQkSQ%2bky70Tw1SszD6GuoylZ859kfbr0CH nkdXR mwxLW7cJtCJym88GmTgsrrExWnNNSNiN61CAkvo 365&E CF=904+F.2d+at+160 904 F.2d at 160 (citation omitted);

*Campbell,*https://apps.fastcase.com/Research/Pages /Document

.aspx?LTID=v%2b%2bWn0pFJOPwVn7bDpURw R5rY%2bX X9Uta8hAwg5stZDj8sEobQkSQ%2bky70Tw1SszD6G uoylZ8 59kfbr0CHnkdXRmwxLW7cJtCJym88GmTgsrrExWn NNSNi N61CAkvo365&ECF=510+U.S.+at+ 510 U.S. at , 114

S.Ct. at 1178 (citing *Fisher v. Dees,* 794 F.2d 432, 438 (9th Cir.1986)).

20. The court notes the difficulty of coming to this conclusion based on the lack of guidance in how to weigh the various factors. *See Rubin v. Brooks/Cole Publishing*

*Co.,*https://apps.fastcase.com/Research/Pages/Document.aspx?
LTID=v%2b%2bWn0pFJOPwVn7bDpURwR5rY%2bX
X9Ut
a8hAwg5stZDj8sEobQkSQ%2bky70Tw1SszD6GuoylZ
859kf
br0CHnkdXRmwxLW7cJtCJym88GmTgsrrExWnNNS
NiN61
CAkvo365&ECF=836+F.Supp.+909%2c+922+%28D.Ma
ss.1

993%29 836 F.Supp. 909, 922 (D.Mass.1993) (citing 3 Nimmer

§ 13.05[A][5], at 13-199).

21. The new Restatement provides a similar definition of a trade secret:

A trade secret is any information that can be used in the operation of a business or other enterprise and that is sufficiently valuable and secret to afford an actual or potential economic advantage over others.

Restatement (Third) of Unfair Competition ("Restatement") § 39, at 425 (1995). Although California has adopted the UTSA, courts also look to the Restatement to help interpret the UTSA. *See* Restatement § 39, cmt. b, at 427; *cf.* 1 Milgrim § 1.01[1], at 1-3 (noting that UTSA jurisdictions frequently rely on the Restatement's definition of a trade secret).

22. In granting summary judgment for the Church on its claim that a splinter group had misappropriated the Advanced Technology works, the Southern District of California did not address this preliminary question of whether religious scriptures should be unprotectable as trade secrets because of their noncommercial, religious nature. *Vien,*https://apps.fastcase.com/Research/Pages

/Document.aspx?LTID=v%2b%2bWn0pFJOPwVn 7bDpURw R5rY%2bXX9Uta8hAwg5stZDj8sEobQkSQ%2bky70T w1Ssz D6GuoylZ859kfbr0CHnkdXRmwxLW7cJtCJym88Gm

TgsrrE
xWnNNSNiN61CAkvo365&ECF=827+F.Supp.+629
827

F.Supp. 629. Instead, the court found that the works were trade secrets because the Church had used reasonable steps to keep the works secret and because they had independent economic value both to plaintiffs, who use the proceeds from the sale of these materials to support the operation of the Church, and to the defendant, who was a competitor of the Church who also charged for Scientology-like courses. *Id.* at 633-34.

23. Neither the Church's status as a religion nor its not-for-profit status are at issue in the current dispute.
24. In a declaration that was prepared in *Church of Scientology Int'l*

v. Fishman, No. 91-6426 HLH (Tx), Erlich cites to books and articles by former Scientologists on the lack of security measures accompanying the study of the Advanced Technology materials. Erlich's Request for Judicial Notice, "Berger Decl.," Exs. 10, 22. This is clearly hearsay if offered to show the truth of the statements that the security measures were inadequate. The court nonetheless notes that the documents confirm that works were taken home in locked bags. *See id.*, Ex. 10, at 30.

25. The notion that the Church's trade secrets are disclosed to thousands of parishioners makes this a rather unusual trade secrets case. However, because parishioners are required to maintain the secrecy of the materials, McShane May 31, 1995 Decl. 3, the court sees no reason why the mere fact that many people have seen the information should negate the information's trade secret status. *See SmokEnders,* https://apps.fastcase.com/Research/Pages/Document.aspx?LTI D=v%2b%2bWn0pFJOPwVn7bDpURwR5rY%2b XX9Uta8h Awg5stZDj8sEobQkSQ%2bky70Tw1SszD6Guoyl Z859kfbr0 CHnkdXRmwxLW7cJtCJym88GmTgsrrExWnN NSNiN61CA kvo365&ECF=184+U.S.P.Q.+at+317 184 U.S.P.Q. at 317 (citing *Chicago Board of Trade v. Christie G & S Co.,* 198 U.S. 236, 25 S.Ct. 637, 49

L.Ed. 1031 (1905)) ("A trade secret owner does not lose his right by communicating the results to persons; even if many, in confidential relations to itself, under a contract not to make public.") While it is logically more likely that a secret will leak out when more people are entrusted with it, absent evidence of leakage the court finds that giving out the secrets to a large number of people, though no more than necessary, is not itself an unreasonable security step.

26. Despite plaintiffs' argument to the contrary, these articles, several of which have been separately authenticated by Erlich's counsel, are not hearsay as they are being offered not for their truth but for the fact that they allegedly disclose to the public RTC's trade secrets.
27. Erlich further cites as relevant authority the Ninth Circuit's observations in its unpublished opinion regarding the confidentiality of the Advanced Technology works. *See*

*Fishman,*https://apps.fastcase.com/Research/Pages/Document.aspx?LTID=v%2b%2bWn0pFJOPwVn7bDpURwR5rY

%2bX X9Uta8hAwg5stZDj8sEobQkSQ%2bky70Tw1SszD6G uoylZ8 59kfbr0CHnkdXRmwxLW7cJtCJym88GmTgsrrExWn NNSNi N61CAkvo365&ECF=1994+WL+467999 1994WL 467999, 1994 U.S.App. LEXIS 23848 (9th Cir. Aug. 30, 1994). This court notes that the Ninth Circuit's Memorandum opinion is not to be cited, except where relevant under the doctrines of law of the case, res judicata, and collateral estoppel. Ninth Cir.Rule 36-

3. It appears that none of the exceptions applies here. Further, the Ninth Circuit made no findings as to the secrecy of the Advanced Technology works, but rather made "observations" that the district court might "wish to take into consideration" on remand.

*Id.*https://apps.fastcase.com/Research/Pages/Document.aspx?L TID=v%2b%2bWn0pFJOPwVn7bDpURwR5rY%2bXX 9Uta8 hAwg5stZDj8sEobQkSQ%2bky70Tw1SszD6GuoylZ85 9kfbr0 CHnkdXRmwxLW7cJtCJym88GmTgsrrExWnNNSNi

N61CA kvo365&ECF=1994+WL+467999 1994 WL467999, at *3, 1994 U.S.App. LEXIS 23848, at *8.

28. There is no merit to Erlich's claim that the registration of the Advanced Technology works with the Copyright Office forfeited their trade secret status, as it appears that these works were registered in masked form. McShane May 31, 1995 Decl., Ex. A. There is likewise no merit to Erlich's argument that the Class VIII Assists lecture tape is not properly licensed to RTC and has not been kept confidential. *See* McShane Depo. at 134, 140; Byrne Decl. ¶¶ 7-14.
29. *See* Trotter Hardy, "The Proper Legal Regime for `Cyberspace'," 55 U.Pitt.L.Rev. 993, 1055 n. 45 (Summer 1994) (noting that "anonymous remailer" exists in Finland to allow anonymous or pseudonymous use of the Internet).
30. *See, e.g.,* McShane May 31, 1995 Decl. ¶ 10. In another case involving some of the same Advanced Technology works, the court found misappropriation of trade secrets where the works were stolen from a Church in Denmark and the defendant's copies must have been

connected to the stolen documents, thereby defeating the defendant's argument that he had acquired the information through proper means. *Religious Technology Center v. Wollersheim,* 228 U.S.P.Q. 534, 536-37, 1985 WL 72663 (C.D.Cal.1985), *rev'd on other grounds,* https://apps.fastcase.com/Research/Pages/Document.aspx?LTI D=v%2b%2bWn0pFJOPwVn7bDpURwR5rY%2b XX9Uta8h Awg5stZDj8sEobQkSQ%2bky70Tw1SszD6Guoyl Z859kfbr0 CHnkdXRmwxLW7cJtCJym88GmTgsrrExWnN NSNiN61CA kvo365&ECF=796+F.2d+1076+%289th+Cir.+1986 %29 796 F.2d 1076 (9th Cir. 1986). The present case is distinguishable because there was no argument in *Wollersheim* that the defendants had received the Church materials in a manner that would destroy their secrecy, i.e., over the Internet or by some other type of publication.

31. Although Erlich does not specifically address the element of misappropriation, the court notes that RTC has shown that Erlich's disclosures over the

> Internet of RTC's Exhibit B works, like that of the defendant in *Vien,* may constitute misappropriation. The fact that Erlich's postings were not of the "entire secret," and included only portions of courses, docs not mean that Erlich's disclosures are not misappropriations. While previous partial disclosures arguably made public only those parts disclosed, Erlich's partial disclosures of non-public portions of the secrets may themselves be actionable because they constitute "disclosure ... without ... consent by a person who ... knew or had reason to know that his... knowledge of the trade secret was ... [either] [d]erived from or through a person who had utilized improper means to acquire it [or] [a]cquired under circumstances giving rise to a duty to maintain its secrecy or limit its use." UTSA § 3426.1(b).

Erlich argues that this case is distinguishable from *Vien* because in *Vien* the defendant was "a competitor of plaintiffs' [sic], who used the Advanced Technology in the delivery of the courses for which she [was] paid" and for which she charged as much as $3000.

*Vien,*https://apps.fastcase.com/Research/Pages/Document.aspx

?LTID=v%2b%2bWn0pFJOPwVn7bDpURwR5rY%2bXX9U

ta8hAwg5stZDj8sEobQkSQ%2bky70Tw1SszD6GuoylZ859kf br0CHnkdXRmwxLW7cJtCJym88GmTgsrrExWnNNSNiN61 CAkvo365&ECF=827+F.Supp.+at+633-34 827 F.Supp. at 633-

34 (emphasis added). Unlike the defendant in *Vien,* Erlich neither offers Scientology-like services nor charges anyone for the use of the materials. Additionally, Erlich seems to argue that his activities are distinguishable from those of the defendants in *Vien* and *Wollersheim* because he never profited from his use of the trade secrets and thus has not misappropriated the works. However, nothing in the UTSA requires that the defendant gain any advantage from the disclosure; it is sufficient to show "use" by disclosure of a trade secret with actual or constructive knowledge that the secret was acquired under circumstances giving rise to a duty to maintain its secrecy. UTSA § 3426.1(b)(2); *Ashton-Tate Corp. v. Ross,*

916 F.2d 516, 523-24 (9th Cir.1990). Thus, Erlich's admitted posting of the information, regardless of any alleged fair use defense or lack of financial motive may constitute misappropriation of the Church's trade secrets.

32. Although there is no evidence that Erlich "copied" item 9 of Exhibits A and B, the court is satisfied that plaintiffs have shown the document to be protectable and of the same nature as other Exhibit A and B documents. Therefore, it is reasonable to include those documents in the injunction.
33. This conclusion, however, is without prejudice to plaintiffs' filing a request for leave to file a supplemental complaint that contains further allegations of infringement of copyright or to request that the preliminary injunction be expanded to cover works which were seized from Erlich and are now being returned. The application would need to show that plaintiffs hold valid copyright interests in the documents.

34. Exhibits A and B, and not Exhibits A-1 and B-1 to the FAC, are the subject of the TRO and the Amended TRO.

35. The writ of seizure provides in relevant part:

TO THE UNITED STATES MARSHAL OR OTHER LAW ENFORCEMENT OFFICERS:

Pursuant to the Order [of February 10, 1995 to Clerk To Issue Writ for Seizure of Articles Infringing Statutory Copyright], which commands me to issue this Writ of Seizure,

YOU ARE DIRECTED to seize, using such force as may be reasonably necessary in the premises, the following articles and things which you may then or otherwise thereafter find on the person, in the possession, or under the control of defendant Dennis Erlich ("Erlich") and/or defendant's agents and persons acting in concert with defendant, at [defendant's home address], or elsewhere where defendant Erlich or any such agents and persons may be found in the territory in which you may serve this Writ, including any building, annex or other structure adjacent to or on the premises identified above, to wit: <u>any and all copies, reproductions, or embodiments of</u>

all or any part of the literary works identified on Exhibits A and B to the Complaint (copies of Exhibits A and B are attached hereto), including any 3½" or 5¼" computer disks and printed materials; all masters and tapes; any articles and things that appear to be works of L. Ron Hubbard protected by copyrights; but excluding all personal computers (including all ancillary equipment and disk drives, found at or within the above-described locations[)].

February 10, 1995 Writ of Seizure (emphasis added).

36. Although Erlich's use of plaintiffs' materials for what is arguably criticism can hardly be analogized to the case of a professional counterfeiter, other considerations make this a good case for ex parte relief. Computer files can be easily uploaded and copied from one location to another and are easy to transport, conceal, or delete. The ability of users to post large amounts of protected works nearly instantaneously over the Internet makes it a rather dangerous haven for copyright infringers.

37. Plaintiffs allege that Erlich has shown his propensity to conceal evidence and lie by his

concealment of the computer containing the infringing materials in a closet in a locked room during the February 13, 1995 seizure. This evidence, which Erlich disputes, is irrelevant to the question of what evidence presented to the court prior to the issuance of the ex parte seizure order showed that the court should dispense with the usual notice requirement. *See First Technology,*https://apps.fastcase.com/Research/Pages/Document.aspx?LTID=v%2b%2bWn0pFJOP wVn7bDpURwR5rY%2bXX9Uta8hAwg5stZDj8s EobQkSQ% 2bky70Tw1SszD6GuoylZ859kfbr0CHnkdXRmw xLW7cJtCJy m88GmTgsrrExWnNNSNiN61CAkvo365&ECF=11+F.3d+at

+651-52 11 F.3d at 651-52.

38. The cases cited by plaintiffs for the proposition that a very broad seizure is justified are not on point. The extremely broad searches and seizures in those cases were justified because of the pervasiveness of the crime or fraud.

39. The court is disturbed by the possibility that plaintiffs copied the entirety of Erlich's hard drive onto a tape for examination at their leisure. If Erlich did not, as he claims, consent to this part of the seizure, this would constitute a significant intrusion into Erlich's private affairs that was not justified by the need to identify infringing copies. *But see* McShane February 21, 1995 Decl. ¶

7 (stating that Erlich consented to plaintiffs' reviewing his floppy disks off the premises if the non-infringing disks were returned). The court is also disturbed by allegations that plaintiffs deleted materials from Erlich's hard drive if such materials were not also saved on floppies or tape back-up for possible later restoration.

40. Erlich's additional arguments are mooted by the court's conclusion. The court has already disposed of Erlich's argument that plaintiffs' failure to prove likelihood of success on the merits and irreparable harm is an independent ground for vacating the writ of seizure. Because the court has determined that the writ of seizure should be vacated, there is no need to consider

Erlich's request to increase the amount of the bond. Erlich's request for the return of certain improperly seized articles is also moot as all materials must be returned.

41. The court notes that plaintiffs are not alone in placing new arguments in their Reply — Erlich's Reply in support of his motion to dissolve the TRO contained several new arguments. The proper response to such new arguments, however, would be to object to the new arguments, not to endlessly continue the arguments back and forth.

CASE SUMMARY

(PAGE 143-163)

Worldwide Church of God v. Philadelphia Church of God, Inc. (2000) - The founder and pastor of the Radio Church of God (later, the Worldwide Church of God), authored over 3,000 articles for the church's magazine and registered the copyright in his work in the church's name. After his death, the church distributed over 1.2 million free copies before it discontinued distribution. The reason for discontinuation was that the church's doctrine had changed and the late pastor's views were outdated and racist in nature. Two former members founded a new religious organization, requiring the reading of the protected work for all its members. It also copied the work verbatim and removed the Worldwide Church of God's name, replacing it with its own, Philadelphia Church of God, Inc. Philadelphia Church of God refused to stop infringing and a copyright infringement lawsuit was filed. The court considered the factors of fair use, but found that the use was infringing.

CASE LAW

WORLDWIDE CHURCH OF GOD, a California Corporation, Plaintiff- Counter-Defendant-Appellant, v. PHILADELPHIA CHURCH OF GOD, INC., an Oklahoma Corporation, Defendant- Counter-Claimant-Appellee.

UNITED STATES COURT OF APPEALS FOR THE NINTH CIRCUIT 227 F.3d 1110; 2000 U.S. App. LEXIS 23390; 56 U.S.P.Q.2D (BNA) 1259; Copy. L. Rep. (CCH) P28,151; 2000 Cal.

Daily Op. Service 7761;2000 Daily Journal DAR 10303

December 6, 1999, Argued and Submitted, Pasadena, California September 18, 2000, Filed

SUBSEQUENT HISTORY:

[*1] Certiorari Denied April 2, 2001, Reported at: **2001 U.S. LEXIS 2734**.

PRIOR HISTORY:

Appeal from the United States District Court Central District of California.

D.C. No. CV-97-05306-JSL. J. Spencer Letts, District Judge Presiding.

DISPOSITION:

Reversed judgment for PCG in Nos. 99-55934 and 99-56489, and denial of WCG's motion for preliminary injunction in No. 99-55850, dismissed appeal from denial of WCG's motion for an injunction pending appeal in No. 99-56005 as moot, and remanded for entry of preliminary injunction pending trial of any damages and final adjudication.

COUNSEL: Allan Browne, Brown & Woods, LLP, Beverly Hills, California, for the plaintiff/counter-defendant-appellant.

Mark B. Helm, Munger, Tolles & Olson, LLP, Los Angeles, California, and Kelly M. Klaus, Munger, Tolles & Olson, LLP, San Francisco, California, for the defendant/counter-claimant-appellee.

JUDGES: Before: Melvin Brunetti and A. Wallace Tashima, Circuit Judges, William W Schwarzer, * Senior District Judge. Opinion by Judge Schwarzer; Dissent by Judge Brunetti.*

The Honorable William W Schwarzer, Senior United States District Judge for the Northern District of California, sitting by designation.

OPINION BY: William W Schwarzer

OPINION

SCHWARZER, Senior District Judge:

Appellant Worldwide [*2] Church of God ("WCG") is a nonprofit religious organization whose late Pastor General, Herbert W. Armstrong, wrote a 380-page book entitled *Mystery of the Ages* ("*MOA*"), the copyright to which is held by WCG. After Armstrong's death, WCG retired *MOA* from distribution and use. Appellee Philadelphia Church of God ("PCG"), also a nonprofit religious organization, then appropriated *MOA* for use in its religious observance, copying it in its entirety and distributing large numbers of copies to its members and the public. We must decide whether PCG's copying and dissemination of *MOA* constitutes fair use under the Copyright Statute. **17 U.S.C. § 107**.

FACTUAL BACKGROUND

Herbert Armstrong founded the Radio Church of God, later renamed Worldwide Church of God, in 1934. He held the title of "Pastor General with the spiritual rank of Apostle" and was its undisputed spiritual and temporal leader until his death in 1986. Armstrong was a prolific writer, producing over three thousand articles for the church's magazine *The Plain Truth,* all of which were copyrighted in the name of WCG, or its affiliate teaching arm, Ambassador College.

Armstrong wrote [*3] *MOA,* his final work, between 1984 and 1985. He completed it when he was ninety-two years old, shortly before his death. He copyrighted it in the name of WCG and published it in serial form in *The Plain Truth* magazine, distributed free of charge to approximately eight million people. In addition, WCG distributed over 1.24 million copies free of charge to employees and to viewers of WCG telecasts. In all, WCG put over nine million free copies of *MOA* into circulation.

Two years after Armstrong's death, WCG decided to discontinue distribution of *MOA* for several reasons, including the fact that the Church's positions on various doctrines such as divorce, remarriage, and divine healing had changed. The Church hoped to "prevent a transgression of conscience by proclaiming what the Church considered to be ecclesiastical error" espoused in *MOA* and it considered that Armstrong, who was ninety- two when he wrote *MOA*, conveyed outdated views that were racist in nature. Its Advisory Council of Elders indicated that the Church stopped distributing *MOA* because of "cultural standards of social sensitivity" and to avoid racial conflict. The Council noted, "Insensitivity [*4] in this area is contrary to the doctrinal program of WCG to promote racial healing and reconciliation among the races." WCG disposed of excess inventory copies of *MOA* and stopped distribution, but retained archival and research copies. WCG never sought to withdraw or destroy personal copies or copies held by public institutions or any public library, nor did it request that its members destroy their copies. WCG has indicated an interest in publishing an annotated *MOA* sometime in the future but has not yet begun work on it.

In 1989, two former WCG ministers, Gerald Flurry and John Amos, founded a new religious organization, PCG. The new church grew to over six thousand members by 1996 and claims strictly to follow the teachings of Herbert Armstrong. PCG asserts that *MOA* is central to its religious practice and required reading for all members hoping to be baptized into PCG. Until January 1997, PCG relied on existing copies of *MOA* but it then began copying *MOA* for its own use. It is undisputed that PCG never requested permission from WCG to print *MOA*. It is also undisputed that PCG copied *MOA* verbatim, deleting only WCG from the copyright page and substituting [*5] Herbert Armstrong in its place, and deleting a "Suggested Reading" page and a warning against reproduction without permission. PCG has distributed approximately thirty thousand copies of its *MOA* in English text, in addition to foreign-language versions. It has advertised its version in newspapers and periodicals and has received substantial contributions from persons who have received its *MOA*.

When PCG ignored WCG's demand that it cease infringing its copyright and continued distribution of its *MOA*, this action followed.

PROCEDURAL BACKGROUND

In its complaint, WCG alleged that PCG, by reproducing, distributing, promoting, advertising and offering unlawful and unauthorized copies of *MOA*, has been infringing WCG's copyright. PCG answered, denying WCG's ownership of the copyright and asserting that WCG's claim was barred by the **Free Exercise Clause of the First Amendment**, the Religious Freedom Restoration Act ("RFRA"), 42 U.S.C. §§ 2000bb- 2000bb-4, and the fair use doctrine, **17 U.S.C. § 107**, and counterclaimed seeking a declaration of its right to reproduce and distribute *MOA*. n1

-------------- Footnotes

The district court granted WCG's motion to strike the RFRA defense and counterclaim before reaching PCG's summary judgment motion. The RFRA issue is before us, therefore, only by way of the appeal from the final judgment.

- - - - - - - - - - - - End Footnotes- - - - - - - - - - - - - -

[*6] WCG moved for partial summary judgment and for a preliminary injunction to restrain PCG from printing or distributing any materials copyrighted by WCG, including *MOA*. PCG filed a cross-motion for summary adjudication. The district court denied WCG's motions and granted PCG's motion for summary adjudication. It concluded that Armstrong was the author of *MOA* and that it was not a work for hire, implying that WCG did not own the copyright, and that PCG's use of *MOA* is statutorily protected "fair use" of the work under **17 U.S.C. § 107**.

WCG appeals the order granting summary judgment to PCG (No. 99- 55934), the denial of its motion for a preliminary injunction (No. 99- 55850), and the denial of its motion to amend the judgment (No. 99- 56005). On June 30, 1999, this court granted the motions to consolidate these three appeals. On July 23, 1999, the district court entered judgment for PCG on WCG's complaint pursuant to **Federal Rule of Civil Procedure 54(b)**. WCG filed a notice of appeal with respect to that judgment (No. 99-56489), and this court granted appellee's motion to consolidate that appeal as well. Because all of the district court's orders are merged [*7] into the final judgment, we have jurisdiction pursuant to **28 U.S.C. § 1291**. We review a grant of summary judgment *de novo*. *See* **Balint v. Carson City, Nevada, 180 F.3d 1047, 1050 (9th Cir. 1999)** (en banc).

DISCUSSION

I. OWNERSHIP OF THE COPYRIGHT

PCG disputes WCG's ownership of the *MOA* copyright, contending that Armstrong, not WCG, had the right to control *MOA*'s creation and that therefore WCG cannot claim either authorship or ownership of *MOA* through the "work-for-hire" doctrine under **17 U.S.C. § 201(b)**, and the district court so found. We need not address this hotly disputed issue, however, for it is undisputed that Armstrong, who owned the copyright, bequeathed his entire estate to WCG. His Will left all of his real and personal property to WCG. The Will was admitted to probate and was not challenged. The Superior Court entered an order of final distribution providing that "preliminary distribution having . . . been made, . . . all other property belonging to said estate . . . be and is hereby distributed to Worldwide Church of God." Because the ownership of a copyright may, under **17 U.S.C. § 201** [*8] **(d)**, "be bequeathed by will," WCG is now the owner.

PCG responds that "Armstrong granted a nonexclusive, implied license for *MOA* to be disseminated by those who value its religious message." As a result, it argues, WCG took any copyright subject to this preexisting license. The existence of a license creates an affirmative defense to a claim of copyright infringement. **I.A.E., Inc. v. Shaver, 74 F.3d 768, 775 (7th Cir. 1996)**, citing **Effects Assoc., Inc. v. Cohen, 908 F.2d 555, 559 (9th Cir. 1990)**. PCG did not plead this defense in its answer (or otherwise raise it in the district court) as required by **Federal Rule of Civil Procedure 8(c)** ("In pleading to a preceding pleading, a party shall set forth affirmatively [the affirmative defense of] . . . license."). Accordingly, the issue is not properly before us. *See*

Magana v. Commonwealth of the N. Mariana Islands, 107 F.3d 1436, 1446 (9th Cir. 1997). In any event, the argument is without merit. An implied license may be granted orally or be implied from conduct.

See **Effects, 908 F.2d at 558**. PCG does not contend that Armstrong granted it a license, but only that [*9] he wished *MOA* to have the largest audience possible. It has offered no evidence that Armstrong created *MOA* for dissemination by third parties, much less that he intended to license PCG to reprint the entire book and use it for its own church. We conclude that Armstrong's copyright passed to WCG through his Will and that WCG is the owner of the copyright in *MOA*.

II. THE "FAIR USE" DEFENSE

A.

The district court concluded that the facts "support a finding that PCG's use of *MOA* is a statutorily protected 'fair use' of the work." In reaching this conclusion, it found that PCG uses *MOA* "for non-profit religious and educational purposes," that copying a complete religious text "is reasonable in relation to that use," that WCG presented no evidence that it lost members due to PCG's distribution, that a potential annotated *MOA* produced by WCG would not compete against PCG's copies of *MOA*, and that *MOA*'s being out of print provided additional justification for PCG's production of *MOA*. WCG contends that the district court's determination of "fair use" is factually and legally erroneous.

Fair use is a mixed question of law and fact. If there are [*10] no genuine issues of material fact, or if, even after resolving all issues in favor of the opposing party, a reasonable trier of fact can reach only one conclusion, a court may conclude as a matter of law whether the challenged use qualifies as a fair use of the copyrighted work. *See* **Hustler Magazine, Inc. v. Moral Majority, Inc., 796 F.2d 1148, 1150-51 (9th Cir. 1986)**. Where the record is sufficient to evaluate each of the statutory factors, "an appellate court 'need not remand for further fact-finding . . . [but] may conclude as a matter of law that the . . . use does not qualify as a fair use of the copyrighted work.'" **Harper & Row, Publishers, Inc. v. Nation Enter., 471 U.S. 539, 560, 85 L. Ed. 2d**

588, 105 S. Ct. 2218 (1985) (quoting Pacific & S. Co. v. Duncan, 744 F.2d 1490, 1495 (11th Cir. 1984)).

Under **§ 106** of the Copyright Act, WCG as the owner of the copyright has the exclusive right to reproduce and distribute copies of *MOA*. **17 U.S.C. § 106(1), (3)**. That right is not diminished or qualified by the fact that WCG is a not-for-profit organization and does not realize monetary benefit from the [*11] use of the copyrighted work. Nor is that right affected by the religious nature of its activity; Congress narrowly limited the privilege accorded religious uses to "performance of a . . . literary or musical work . . . or display of a work, in the course of services at a place of worship or other religious assembly." **17 U.S.C. § 110(3)**. PCG's unauthorized copying and distribution of *MOA* falls outside of that narrow exception to copyright protection. *See* **F.E.L. Publications, Ltd. v. Catholic Bishop of Chicago, 1982 U.S. App. LEXIS 20700, 214 U.S.P.Q. 409, 411, 1982 WL 19198**

(7th Cir.) ("F.E.L can prevent churches from copying or publishing its copyrighted works, even if the churches only intend to use the copies or publications at not-for-profit religious services Neither the religious element nor the non-profit element of a performance will protect illegal copying or publishing."). We have held that we must be careful not to deprive religious organizations of all recourse to the protections of civil law that are available to all others. Such a deprivation would raise its own serious problems under the **Free Exercise Clause** [citation [*12] omitted]. It would also leave religious organizations at the mercy of anyone who appropriated their property with an assertion of religious right to it.

Maktab Tarighe Oveyssi Shah Maghsoudi, Inc. v. Kianfar, 179 F.3d 1244, 1248 (9th Cir. 1999).

Nor do **First Amendment** free speech considerations support PCG's claim of fair use based on WCG's withdrawal of *MOA* from distribution.

The public interest in the free flow of information is assured by the law's refusal to recognize a valid copyright in facts. The fair use doctrine is not a license for corporate theft, empowering a court to ignore a copyright whenever it determines the underlying work contains material of possible public importance.

Harper & Row, 471 U.S. at 558 (quoting Iowa State Univ. Research Found., Inc. v. American Broad. Cos., Inc., 621 F.2d 57, 61 (2d Cir. 1980)). "Moreover, freedom of thought and expression 'includes both the right to speak freely and the right to refrain from speaking at all.'" Id. 471 U.S. at 559 (quoting Wooley v. Maynard, 430 U.S. 705, 714, 51 L. Ed. 2d 752, 97 S. Ct. 1428 (1977)); *see also* Salinger

v. Random House, Inc., 811 F.2d 90, 100 (2d Cir. 1987) [*13] (holding that copyright owner has right to protect "the expressive content of his unpublished writings for the term of his copyright"). This is not a case of "abuse of the copyright owner's monopoly as an instrument to suppress facts." Harper & Row, 471 U.S. at 559. *Cf.* Rosemont Enter., Inc. v.

Random House, Inc., 366 F.2d 303, 311 (2d Cir. 1966) (concurring opinion) (purchase by Howard Hughes of copyright on magazine articles to block publication of his biography). As the Supreme Court has explained:

Although dissemination of creative works is a goal of the Copyright Act, the Act creates a balance between the artist's right to control the work during the term of the copyright protection and the public's need for access to creative works. The copyright term is limited so that the public will not be permanently deprived of the fruits of an artist's labors. [Citation omitted]. But nothing in the copyright statutes would prevent an author from hoarding all of his works during the term of the copyright. **Stewart v. Abend, 495 U.S. 207, 228-29, 109 L. Ed. 2d 184, 110 S. Ct. 1750 (1990)**.

B.

PCG seeks to defend its infringing [*14] activity as fair use under **§ 107** of the Copyright Act. That section provides in relevant part that "the fair use of a copyrighted work . . . for purposes such as criticism, comment, news reporting, teaching . . .,scholarship or research, is not an infringement of copyright." **17 U.S.C. § 107**. In determining whether the use made of a work in any particular case is a fair use, **§ 107** provides that the factors to be considered shall include:

1. the purpose and character of the use, including whether such use is of a commercial nature or is for nonprofit educational purposes;
2. the nature of the copyrighted work; (3) the amount and substantiality of the portion used in relation to the copyrighted work as a whole; and (4) the effect of the use upon the potential market for or value of the copyrighted work.**17 U.S.C. § 107**.

The common-law background of the fair use doctrine illuminates the consideration of the factors Congress incorporated into **§ 107**. As the Supreme Court has explained:

The statutory formulation of the defense of fair use in the Copyright Act reflects the intent of Congress to codify the common-law [*15] doctrine. .. . "The author's consent to a reasonable use of his copyrighted works had always been implied by the courts as a necessary incident of the constitutional policy of promoting the progress of science and the useful arts, since a prohibition of such use would inhibit subsequent writers from attempting to improve upon prior works and thus . . . frustrate the very ends sought to be attained." [Ball, Law of Copyright and Literary Property 260 (1944)]. Professor Latman, in a study of the doctrine of fair use commissioned by Congress for the revision effort, see [**Sony Corp.** **v.**

Universal City Studios, Inc., 464 U.S. 417, 462-463 n.9, 78 L. Ed. **2d 574, 104 S. Ct. 774** (dissenting opinion)], summarized prior law as turning on the "importance of the material copied or performed from the point of view of the reasonable copyright owner. In other words, would the reasonable copyright owner have consented to the use?" **Harper & Row, 471 U.S. at 549-50**.

The Court went on to observe that Justice Story gave early judicial recognition to the doctrine, quoting the following statement: reviewer may fairly cite largely from the original [*16] work, if his design be really and truly to use the passages for the purposes of fair and reasonable criticism. On the other hand, it is as clear, that if he thus cites the most important parts of the work, with a view, not to criticize, but to supersede the use of the original work, and substitute the review for it, such a use will be deemed in law a piracy. **Id. at 550** (quoting **Folsom v. Marsh, 9 F. Cas. 342, 344- 45 (C.C. Mass. 1841))**.

C.

With this background in mind, we turn to consideration of the four statutory factors.

1. The first factor calls for consideration of "the purposes and character of the use, including whether such use is of a commercial nature or is for nonprofit educational purposes." **17 U.S.C. § 107(1)**. "The central purpose of this investigation is to see, in Justice Story's words, whether the new work merely 'supersedes the objects' of the original creation [citations omitted] or instead adds something new, with a further purpose or different character, altering the first with new expression, meaning, or message; it asks, in other words, whether and to what extent the new work is 'transformative. [*17] '" **Campbell v. Acuff-Rose Music, Inc., 510 U.S. 569, 579, 127 L. Ed. 2d 500, 114 S. Ct. 1164 (1994)**. As Justice Story put it:

> "There must be real, substantial condensation of the materials, and intellectual labor and judgment bestowed thereon; and not merely the facile use of the scissors; or extracts of the essential parts, constituting the chief value of the original work." **Folsom, 9 F. Cas. at 345**.

PCG's copying of WCG's *MOA* in its entirety bespeaks no "intellectual labor and judgment." It merely "supersedes the object" of the original *MOA*, to serve religious practice and education. Although "transformative use is not absolutely necessary for a finding of fair use," **Campbell, 510 U.S. at 579**, where the "use is for the same intrinsic purpose as [the copyright holder's] . . . such use seriously weakens a claimed fair use." **Weissmann v. Freeman, 868 F.2d 1313, 1324 (2d Cir. 1989)**.

Nevertheless, PCG argues that this factor favors fair use because its use is not commercial or for profit. The Supreme Court has cautioned that "the commercial or nonprofit educational purpose of a work is only one element of the [*18] first factor inquiry into its purpose and character." **Campbell, 510 U.S. at 584**. While the fact that a publication is commercial tends to weigh against fair use, the absence of a commercial use merely eliminates the presumption of unfairness. "The mere fact that a use is educational and not for profit does not insulate it from a finding of infringement " *Id.*;

see also **Sony Corp. v. Universal City Studios, Inc., 464 U.S. 417, 450, 78 L. Ed. 2d 574, 104 S. Ct. 774 (1984)** ("Even copying for noncommercial purposes may impair the copyright holder's ability to obtain the rewards that Congress intended him to have."); **Marcus v. Rowley, 695 F.2d 1171, 1175 (9th Cir. 1983)**. "The crux of the profit/nonprofit distinction is not whether the sole motive of the use is monetary gain but whether the user stands to profit from exploitation of the copyrighted material without paying the customary price." **Harper & Row, 471 U.S. at 562**. We agree with the Second Circuit that in weighing whether the purpose was for "profit," "monetary gain is not the sole criterion . . . particularly in [a] . . . setting [where] profit [*19] is ill-measured in dollars." **Weissmann, 868 F.2d at 1324** (holding that a professor's verbatim copying of an academic work was not fair use, in part because "the profit/nonprofit distinction is context specific, not dollar dominated" and a professor can "profit" by gaining recognition among his peers and authorship credit). *See also* Webster's Third New International Dictionary (1971) 1811 (defining "profit" as "an advantage, [a] benefit").

Putting aside the disputed question whether PCG uses *MOA* to generate income, and having in mind that like academia, religion is generally regarded as "not dollar dominated," *MOA*'s use unquestionably profits PCG by providing it at no cost with the core text essential to its members' religious observance, by attracting through distribution of *MOA* new members who tithe ten percent of their income to PCG, and by enabling the ministry's growth. During the time of PCG's production and distribution of copies of *MOA* its membership grew to some seven thousand members. It is beyond dispute that PCG "profited" from copying *MOA* - it gained an "advantage" or "benefit" from its distribution and use of *MOA* without [*20] having to account to the copyright holder. The first factor weighs against fair use.

2. The second statutory factor, "the nature of the copyrighted work," turns on whether the work is informational or creative. *See* **Harper & Row, 471 U.S. at 563** ("The law generally recognizes a greater need to disseminate factual works than works of fiction or fantasy."); *see also* **Sony, 464 U.S. at 455 n.40** ("Copying a news broadcast may have a stronger claim to fair use than copying a motion picture."); **Hustler, 796 F.2d at 1153-54** ("The scope of fair use is greater when 'informational' as opposed to more 'creative' works are involved."). PCG's brief describes *MOA* as "primarily a textual, historical account of [Armstrong's] views of the 'the truth' of the Bible." While it may be viewed as "factual" by readers who share Armstrong's religious beliefs, the creativity, imagination and originality embodied in *MOA* tilt the scale against fair use. *See* **Dr. Seuss Enter., L.P. v. Penguin Books USA, Inc., 109 F.3d 1394, 1402 (9th Cir. 1997)**.

3. The third factor directs us to consider "the amount and substantiality of the portion used [*21] in relation to the copyrighted work as a whole." **17 U.S.C. § 107(3)**. PCG copied the entire *MOA* verbatim, deleting only the "Suggested Readings" and the reference to "Worldwide

Church of God" from the copyright page. While "wholesale copying does not preclude fair use per se," copying an entire work "militates against a finding of fair use." **Hustler, 796 F.2d at 1155**. Moreover, "the fact that a substantial portion of the infringing work was copied verbatim is evidence of the qualitative value of the copied material, both to the originator and to the plagiarist who seeks to profit from marketing someone else's copyrighted expression." **Harper & Row, 471 U.S. at 565**.

PCG argues its verbatim copying of the whole work is reasonable because its use of *MOA* is religious in nature. "The extent of permissible copying varies with the purpose and character of the use." **Campbell, 510 U.S. at 586-87**. In *Campbell,* the Court held that "copying does not become excessive in relation to parodic purpose merely because the portion taken was the original's heart." **Id. at 588**. PCG's copying stands on a [*22] different footing for the purpose for which it uses the *MOA* is the same as WCG's. This court has held "that a finding that the alleged infringers copied the material to use it for the same intrinsic purpose for which the copyright owner intended it to be used is strong indicia of no fair use." **Marcus, 695 F.2d at 1175**. Reliance on *Sony* would be misplaced. There, the Supreme Court held that reproduction of the entire work "[did] not have its ordinary effect of militating against a finding of fair use" under the unique circumstances of that case, to wit: copying of videotapes for time-shifting for personal use to "enable[] a viewer to see such a work which he had been invited to witness in its entirety free of charge." **Sony, 464 U.S. at 449-50**. No such circumstances exist here to justify PCG's reproduction of the entire work. PCG uses the *MOA* as a central element of its members' religious observance; a reasonable person would expect PCG to pay WCG for the right to copy and distribute *MOA* created by WCG with its resources. The third factor, therefore, weighs against fair use.

1. The fourth factor considers "the effect of the use [*23] upon the potential market for or value of the copyrighted work." **17 U.S.C. § 107(4)**. It has been said that "fair use, when properly applied, is limited to copying by others which does not

materially impair the marketability of the work which is copied." **Harper & Row, 471 U.S. at 566-67** (quoting **Nimmer, Copyright § 1.10[D]**, at 1-87). This case presents a novel application of the fair use doctrine where the copyright owner is a not-for-profit organization. As might be expected, published case law deals with works marketed for profit. However, it cannot be inferred from that fact that the absence of a conventional market for a work, the copyright to which is held by a nonprofit, effectively deprives the holder of copyright protection. If evidence of actual or potential monetary loss were required, copyrights held by nonprofits would be essentially worthless. Religious, educational and other public interest institutions would suffer if their publications invested with an institution's reputation and goodwill could be freely appropriated by anyone.

The statute by its terms is not limited to market effect but includes also "the effect of the use [*24] on the *value* of the copyrighted work." **17 U.S.C. § 107(4)** (emphasis added). As *Sony* states, "even copying for noncommercial purposes may impair the copyright holder's ability to obtain the rewards that Congress intended him to have." **Sony, 464 U.S. at 450**. Those rewards need not be limited to monetary rewards; compensation may take a variety of forms. **Id. at 447 n.28** ("The copyright law does not require a copyright owner to charge a fee for the use of his works. It is not the role of the courts to tell copyright holders the best way for them to exploit their copyrights").

WCG points out that those who respond to PCG's ads are the same people who would be interested in WCG's planned annotated version or any future republication of the original version. With an annotated *MOA,* WCG hopes to reach out to those familiar with Armstrong's teachings and those in the broader Christian community. PCG's distribution of its unauthorized version of *MOA* thus harms WCG's goodwill by diverting potential members and contributions from WCG. While the district court found that PCG's *MOA* and WCG's proposed annotated [*25] *MOA* "would not in any sense 'compete' in the same market," undisputed evidence shows that individuals who received copies of *MOA* from PCG are present or could be potential adherents of WCG. *MOA*'s value is as a marketing device; that is how PCG uses it and both PCG and WCG are engaged in evangelizing in the Christian community.

PCG argues that WCG's failure to exploit *MOA* for ten years and its lack of a concrete plan to publish a new version show that "*MOA* has no economic value to the WCG that the PCG's dissemination of the work would adversely affect." We disagree. Even an author who had disavowed any intention to publish his work during his lifetime was entitled to protection of his copyright, first, because the relevant consideration was the "potential market" and, second, because he has the right to change his mind. *See* **Salinger, 811 F.2d at 99**. WCG explained that it ceased distribution because the Church's position on various doctrines had changed, continued distribution would offend cultural standards of social sensitivity, and dissemination would perpetuate what the Church considered ecclesiastical error. For those reasons, WCG planned an [*26] annotated edition of *MOA*. n2

- - - - - - - - - - - - - - Footnotes 2

Because the Church plans at some time to publish an annotated version of *MOA,* it is entitled to protection of its copyright. This is not a case of market failure, as PCG contends, for the very reason stated in the article on which it relies:

When an owner refuses to license because he is concerned that defendant's work will substitute for his own work or derivative works, the owner is representing not only his own interest, but also the interest of his potential customers and thus the public interest. Market failure should be found only when the defendant can prove that the copyright owner would refuse to license out of a desire unrelated to the goals of copyright - notably a desire to keep certain information from the public.Wendy Gordon, *Fair Use As Market Failure: A Structural and Economic Analysis of the Betamax Case and its Predecessors,* **82 Colum. L. Rev. 1600, 1634 (1982)**.

------------- End Footnotes--------------

Finally, PCG argues that if WCG published an annotated version [*27] it would be so different as not to be competitive with PCG's *MOA*. The argument, aside from being speculative, misses the point. The fact remains that PCG has unfairly appropriated *MOA* in its entirety for the very purposes for which WCG created *MOA*. We have found no published case holding that fair use protected the verbatim copying, without criticism, of a written work in its entirety. As the 1967 House Report notes, the market factor "must almost always be judged in conjunction with the other three criteria." H.R. Rep. No. 83, at 35 (1967). Judge Pierre N. Leval has written:

When the secondary use does substantially interfere with the market for the copyrighted work, as was the case in [*Harper & Row*], this factor powerfully opposes a finding of fair use. But the inverse does not follow. The fact that the secondary use does not harm the market for the original gives no assurance that the secondary use is justified. Thus, notwithstanding the importance of the market factor, especially when the market is impaired by the secondary use, it should not overshadow the requirement of justification under the first factor, without which there can be no fair use.

[*28] Pierre N. Leval, *Toward a Fair Use Standard,* **103 Harv. L. Rev. 1105, 1124 (1990)**.

On balance, the defense of fair use of *MOA* fails. The first three factors weigh in WCG's favor and the fourth factor is, at worst, neutral.

III. PCG's DEFENSE UNDER THE RELIGIOUS FREEDOM RESTORATION ACT

PCG contends that the judgment should be affirmed on the independent ground of the Religious Freedom Restoration Act ("RFRA"), 42 U.S.C. §§ 2000bb-2000bb-4. RFRA provides in relevant part that "Government shall not substantially burden a person's exercise of religion even if the burden results from a rule of general applicability [subject to exceptions not relevant here]." **42 U.S.C. § 2000bb-1(a)**. RFRA "essentially requires the government to justify any regulation imposing a substantial burden on the free exercise of religion by showing that the regulation satisfies strict scrutiny." **Goehring v. Brophy, 94 F.3d 1294, 1298 n.4 (9th Cir. 1996)**. PCG contends that the relief requested by WCG would substantially burden a central tenet of its religious doctrine, namely, distribution of *MOA* to current [*29] and potential adherents of its church. It also considers *MOA* to play an important role in its daily religious practice. The district court dismissed PCG's claim and affirmative defense under RFRA.

In **City of Boerne v. Flores, 521 U.S. 507, 138 L. Ed. 2d 624, 117 S. Ct. 2157 (1997)**, the Supreme Court held that RFRA exceeded the authority of Congress under **Section 5 of the Fourteenth Amendment** to enforce the **First Amendment**. We have held, along with most other courts, that the Supreme Court invalidated RFRA only as applied to state and local law.

See **Sutton v. Providence St. Joseph Med. Ctr., 192 F.3d 826, 832 (9th Cir. 1999)**. We will continue to assume, without deciding, that RFRA is constitutional as applied to federal law. *See* **id. at 833-34**. Courts have interpreted RFRA as an amendment of existing federal statutes and thus a constitutional exercise of Congressional authority. In **In re Young, 141 F.3d 854 (8th Cir. 1998)**, the court found RFRA amended the bankruptcy code, precluding the bankruptcy trustee from avoiding a debtor's tithes to his church. **Id. at 861**. *See also* **EEOC v. Catholic Univ. of Am., 317 U.S. App. D.C. 343, 83 F.3d 455, 470 (D.C. Cir. 1996)** [*30] (holding, pre-

Boerne, that RFRA precluded application of Title VII to plaintiff whose position was the functional equivalent of a minister).

Whether the rationale of those cases can be extended to the copyright statute is an open question. It seems unlikely that the government action Congress envisioned in adopting RFRA included the protection of intellectual property rights against unauthorized appropriation. *Compare* **International Olympic Comm. v. San Francisco Arts & Athletics, 781 F.2d 733, 737 (9th Cir. 1986)** (enforcement of federally-granted trademarks is not state action). We need not decide this knotty question, however, for in the context of this case PCG has failed to demonstrate that the copyright laws subject it to a substantial burden in the exercise of its religion. *See* **United States v. Grant, 117 F.3d 788, 792 n.6 (5th Cir.**

1997) (declining to address constitutionality of RFRA as applied to federal law because the government action at issue did not substantially burden the defendant's free exercise of religion). In its answer to the amended complaint, PCG admitted that it did not seek WCG's permission before copying

MOA. This [*31] fact is confirmed by the certified minutes of the Advisory Council of Elders of the Church of God, submitted under the affidavit of the Secretary of the Church in support of WCG's motion for partial summary judgment, which states: "Prior to January, 1997, neither PCG, nor any of its agents, ever made an offer to purchase the copyrights of the MOA, or any of the Literary Works, nor did they request to purchase a license to exploit any rights therein, nor offered any royalties to do so."

A substantial burden "must be more than an inconvenience." **Bryant v. Gomez, 46 F.3d 948, 949 (9th Cir. 1995)** (quoting **Graham v. C.I.R., 822 F.2d 844, 850-51 (9th Cir. 1987)** (internal citations omitted), *aff'd sub nom.* **Hernandez v. Commissioner, 490 U.S. 680, 699, 104 L. Ed. 2d 766,**

109 S. Ct. 2136 (1988)).

The religious adherent, . . . has the obligation to prove that a governmental regulatory mechanism burdens the adherent's practice of his or her religion by pressuring him or her to commit an act forbidden by the religion or by preventing him or her from engaging in conduct or having a religious experience which the faith mandates. This interference [*32] must be more than an inconvenience; *the burden must be substantial and an interference with a tenet or belief that is central to religious doctrine.*

Goehring, 94 F.3d at 1299 (citation omitted) (alteration and emphasis in the original). Having to ask for permission, and presumably to pay for the right to use an owner's copyrighted work may be an inconvenience, and perhaps costly, but it cannot be assumed to be as a matter of law a substantial burden on the exercise of religion. In the absence of evidence that PCG's needs could not reasonably be accommodated under the copyright laws, we decline to hold that enforcement of those laws in these circumstances constitutes an unreasonable burden. n3

- - - - - - - - - - - - - - Footnotes 3

Because we decide that PCG has not met RFRA's substantial burden test, we need not decide whether the Copyright Act is the least restrictive means of serving a compelling governmental interest. *See* **42 U.S.C. § 2000bb- 1(b)**.

- - - - - - - - - - - - End Footnotes- - - - - - - - - - - - - -

IV. CONCLUSION

The undisputed [*33] facts establish as a matter of law that PCG is not entitled to claim fair use. Because infringement by PCG of WCG's copyright is undisputed, barring fair use, WCG is entitled to a permanent injunction against the reproduction and distribution by PCG of *MOA*. Accordingly, we reverse the judgment for PCG in Nos. 99-55934 and 99- 56489, and the denial of WCG's motion for a preliminary injunction in No. 99-55850, dismiss the appeal from the denial of WCG's motion for an injunction pending appeal in No. 99-56005 as moot, and remand for entry of a preliminary injunction pending a trial of any damages and final adjudication.

Costs on appeal to WCG. SO ORDERED. **DISSENT BY:** Melvin Brunetti DISSENT

BRUNETTI, Circuit Judge, dissenting:

I respectfully dissent and disagree with the majority's reversal of the district court's ruling on fair use.

The copyright dispute in this case arises from a change in religious doctrine of the Worldwide Church of God ("WCG"). This doctrinal shift produced a splinter church, the Philadelphia Church of God ("PCG"). PCG, which was founded by "defrocked" WCG ministers in 1989, seeks to adhere to WCG's original religious doctrine as espoused by its former leader [*34] Herbert W. Armstrong. In particular, PCG views *Mystery of the Ages* ("*MOA*"), a book written by Armstrong, as a divinely inspired text necessary for proper interpretation of the Bible. It is required reading for every member baptized into the PCG church and any prospective member prior to their attendance at church services.

WCG, on the other hand, has renounced many of Armstrong's teachings since shortly after his death in 1986. Although it had previously distributed approximately 1.25 million copies of *MOA* in book form and 8 million copies in serial form, WCG ceased publication and distribution of *MOA* in 1988. WCG then destroyed all excess copies of *MOA* in its inventory, retaining only archival and research copies. WCG has not printed or distributed any copies of *MOA* since 1988 and has no plans for publication or distribution of the work as originally written.

WCG took this course of action, at least in part, because it believes that *MOA* contains historical, doctrinal and social errors. Armstrong's successor at WCG explained that WCG has kept *MOA* out of print based on a "Christian duty" to keep Armstrong's doctrinal errors out of circulation.

WCG has [*35] described *MOA* as "not in conformity with biblical teaching" and "racist." Although WCG claims that it plans to publish an annotated version of *MOA*, as of 1998, a decade after it ceased publishing *MOA*, testimony of WCG leaders demonstrates that the annotation of *MOA* is "not something that is going to be decided or happen any time soon." Apart from determining whether an annotation is financially feasible, WCG would need to take surveys of its membership, assess its priorities, determine the format, hire an author and researcher, and secure a publisher before any such annotation of *MOA* could be published.

PCG was founded because its ministers and members believe the religious doctrine espoused by Armstrong and as set forth in *MOA*. When WCG changed its church doctrine and renounced much of

Armstrong's teachings, the founders and believers of PCG were forced from WCG as they could no longer practice their religious beliefs as set forth in *MOA*. It was WCG's doctrinal shift and renunciations that created the PCG and its need to publish *MOA*.

In light of these facts, this court must decide whether PCG's publication and distribution of *MOA* to church members [*36] and the public without charge beginning in January 1997 constitutes fair use of WCG's copyrighted work.

The fair use doctrine is an equitable rule of reason. **Sony Corp. of America v. Universal City Studios, Inc., 464 U.S. 417, 448** & n.31, **78 L. Ed. 2d 574, 104 S. Ct. 774 (1984)**. The statutory factors listed in **17 U.S.C. § 107** provide guidance in determining when the fair use doctrine applies.

However, there are no bright-line rules and "each case raising the [fair use] question must be decided on its own facts." **Id. at 448 n.31** (quoting H.Rep. No. 94-1476). All four statutory factors "are to be explored, and the results weighed together, in light of the purposes of copyright." **Campbell v.**

Acuff-Rose Music, Inc., 510 U.S. 569, 578, 127 L. Ed. 2d 500, 114

S. Ct. 1164 (1994).

Here, PCG, a nonprofit organization, copied and distributed *MOA* free of charge to spread a religious message. PCG began publishing *MOA* because it was out of print and difficult to obtain through normal channels. It is undisputed that PCG did not solicit any funds in connection with its distribution of *MOA*. PCG's use stands in [*37] sharp contrast to other uses found to be commercial under the first statutory factor. *See* **Campbell, 510 U.S. at 583-85** (parodic rap song sold to the public); **Harper & Row Publishers, Inc. v. Nation Enterprises, 471 U.S. 539, 562, 85 L. Ed. 2d**

588, 105 S. Ct. 2218 (1985) (magazine printed excerpts of soon-to- be published presidential memoir); **Dr. Seuss Enterprises L.P. v. Penguin Books USA, Inc., 109 F.3d 1394, 1403** (9th Cir.), *cert. dismissed,* **118 S. Ct. 27 (1997)** (book-length parody of O.J. Simpson murder trial written in style of Dr. Seuss and intended for public sale); **Hustler Magazine, Inc. v. Moral Majority, Inc., 796 F.2d 1148, 1152-53 (9th**

Cir. 1986) (magazine's parody of prominent minister mailed to minister's supporters together with letters soliciting donations and displayed on television as part of a fundraising drive).

Despite PCG's nonprofit status, its free-of-charge distribution of *MOA*, and the religious purpose behind such distribution, the majority concludes that the first statutory factor militates against a finding of fair use because PCG's use is not transformative and PCG [*38] profits by using *MOA* as a marketing tool to attract new tithing members. As an initial matter, PCG's use need not be transformative to qualify as fair use. **Campbell, 510 U.S. at 579**. In this case, altering or adding to *MOA* would defeat PCG's religious purpose because it believes that *MOA* is a divinely inspired text. As to the profitability of PCG's use, WCG does not contest PCG's assertion that unsolicited donations in response to the distribution of *MOA* fail to come close to covering the enormous expense of printing *MOA*. WCG itself has stated that the costly production of *MOA* was one of the reasons it ceased publication. In my view, the noncommercial and religious elements of PCG's use overwhelm any commercial aspects and weigh in favor of fair use under the first statutory factor. Moreover, the fact that *MOA* had been out of print for nine years at the time of PCG's publication and could only be obtained through some libraries and used bookstores also supports a finding of fair use under the first factor. *See* **Harper & Row, 471 U.S. at 553** ("A key, though not necessarily determinative factor in fair use is whether or not [*39] the work is available to the potential user. If the work is out of print and unavailable for purchase through normal channels, the user may have more justification for reproducing it ") (quoting S.Rep.

No. 94-473 (1975)); **Maxtone-Graham v. Burtchaell, 803 F.2d**

1253, 1264 n.8 (2d Cir. 1986) (out-of-print status of copyrighted book supports fair use determination).

The second and third statutory factors are mostly irrelevant to this case. For example, as a religious text, Armstrong's *MOA* defies easy classification under the second factor as either informational or creative. *Compare* **New Era Publications, Int'l v. Carol Publishing Group, 904 F.2d 152, 157 (2d Cir. 1990)** ("the quoted works - which deal with [Scientology founder L. Ron] Hubbard's life, his views on religion, human relations, the Church, etc. - are more properly viewed as factual or informational") *and* **Religious Technology Center v. Netcom On-Line Com. Services, Inc., 923 F. Supp. 1231, 1246 (N.D. Cal. 1995)** (policy letters of Hubbard Communication Office and works which are part of the methodology of "applied religious philosophy" are primarily functional or [*40] instructive, but other Hubbard works which appear more creative or original deserve greater fair use protection) *with* **Bridge Publications, Inc. v. Vien, 827 F. Supp. 629, 635-36 (S.D. Cal. 1993)** ("the undisputed evidence shows that L. Ron Hubbard's works are the product of his creative thought process, and not merely informational"). As to the amount of copying, even wholesale copying does not weigh against a finding of fair use under the third factor if it is consistent with the noncommercial purpose and character of the use. **Sony, 464 U.S. at 449-50**. In contrast to *Hustler* where the purposes of raising funds and rebutting derogatory information could have been served by less than wholesale copying of the parody, PCG's purpose in seeking to spread the religious message of Armstrong's divinely inspired text, like the nonprofit purpose of home videotaping in *Sony Corp.*, requires copying of the text as a whole. Accordingly, neither the second nor the third statutory factor militate against a finding of fair use.

Even though PCG's use is primarily noncommercial and religious, such use could not be considered fair use in light of the fourth and [*41] most important statutory factor if it impaired the value or marketability of WCG's original *MOA* or its proposed annotated *MOA*. Yet, WCG has intentionally kept *MOA* out of circulation and made no reasonable effort to create an annotated version of *MOA* in the decade following its decision to cease publication. WCG originally distributed *MOA* free of charge as a way of spreading the religious message of its then current leader Armstrong.

Like PCG, WCG used *MOA* as an educational and evangelical tool and may have obtained an indirect financial benefit by attracting tithing members. WCG's decision to cease publication of *MOA*, destroy inventory copies, and disavow *MOA*'s religious message in the context of its doctrinal shift as a church demonstrates that *MOA* is no longer of value to WCG for such purposes, regardless of PCG's actions. Because WCG has admitted that it has no plans to publish or distribute *MOA* as originally written, there can be no market interference.

Nor has WCG shown that "some meaningful likelihood of future harm exists" as to the potential market for WCG's planned publication of an annotated version of *MOA*. *See* **Sony Corp., 464 U.S. at 451**. [*42] In **Maxtone-Graham v. Burtchaell, 803 F.2d 1253 (2d Cir. 1986)**, the court determined that publication of a book opposing abortion which used quotations from an earlier book tending to view abortion in a favorable light did not economically harm the earlier work. The court held that the plans for a second edition of the earlier work was not affected by the publication of the infringing work in part because "it is unthinkable that potential customers for a series of sympathetic interviews on abortion and adoption would withdraw their requests [for a second edition] because a small portion of the work was used in an essay sharply critical of abortion." **Id. at 1264**. It continued by stating that "this conclusion is supported by our finding that the two works served fundamentally different functions, by virtue both of their opposing viewpoints and disparate editorial formats." *Id.*

Here, as in *Maxtone-Graham*, the functions served by *MOA* and the proposed annotation as well as their potential markets are different. In contrast to PCG's evangelical use, the central purpose behind WCG's proposed annotated version of *MOA* is to identify Armstrong's [*43] historical, doctrinal, and social errors. The target markets for the two versions of *MOA* are different because it simply does not make sense for WCG to widely distribute an annotated *MOA* highlighting the errors of the original *MOA* to the general public in order to recruit new members. Unlike a publication which would provide a straight-forward explanation of WCG's religious doctrines for the purposes of recruitment, an annotated version of *MOA* would require a reader to become familiar with the text of the original *MOA* and then to read WCG's response to or criticism of Armstrong's religious views in order to discover WCG's doctrines. Indeed, because WCG hopes to use an annotated *MOA* to reach out to those familiar with Armstrong's teachings, PCG's use creates a larger potential market for an annotation rather than interfering with it. Moreover, the failure of WCG to make any reasonable progress on the annotation over the course of a decade as well as WCG's belief that it has a Christian duty to keep Armstrong's doctrinal errors out of circulation tends to undermine the credibility of WCG's intention to publish any such annotation.

Because there is no evidence, [*44] beyond the mere speculation by WCG's leaders, that PCG's use has a "demonstrable effect on the potential market for, or value of," *MOA* or WCG's proposed annotation, the use "need not be prohibited in order to protect the author's incentive to create." **Sony Corp., 464 U.S. at 450**. The prohibition of PCG's noncommercial, religious use "would merely inhibit access to ideas without any countervailing benefit." **Id. at 450-51**. Accordingly, the fourth statutory factor also supports a finding of fair use.

In this lawsuit, WCG appears less interested in protecting its rights to exploit *MOA* than in suppressing Armstrong's ideas which now run counter to church doctrine. Although the Supreme

Court has recognized that "freedom of thought and expression 'includes both the right to speak freely and the right to refrain from speaking at all,'" it does not "suggest that this right not to speak would sanction an abuse of the copyright owner's monopoly as an instrument to suppress facts." **Harper & Row, 471 U.S. at 559**.

In light of this principle and the statutory factors discussed above, I conclude that the district court did not err in granting [*45] partial summary judgment to PCG because it properly found that PCG's distribution of *MOA* constitutes fair use.

CASE SUMMARY

(PAGES 165-178)

Self-Realization Fellowship Church v. Ananda Church of Self Realization (2000) – Paramahansa Yogananda, the founder of the Self-Realization Fellowship Church (SRF) wrote articles, books, and recorded lectures. His vow of poverty led him to assign all of his possessions to SRF. Ten years after his death, a rival church dedicated to Yogananda's teachings copied the books, articles, and recordings. One of the questions presented was whether Yogananda's work was a "work for hire" owned by the (church) corporation, or whether he was an independent contractor and therefore owned his works. As an independent contractor for SRF, the rights would have been retained by Yogananda, then reverted to his family for the renewal period provided by copyright law. The court held that the work was not "work for hire" and Yogananda retained his intellectual property rights.

CASE LAW

SELF-REALIZATION FELLOWSHIP CHURCH, a California

corporation,

Plaintiff-Appellant, v.

ANANDA CHURCH OF SELF-REALIZATION, a California corporation; Fellowship of Inner Communion, a California corporation; James Walters, aka Sri Kriyananda, Defendants- Appellees.

No. 97-17407.

Argued and Submitted Feb. 15, 2000.

Decided March 23, 2000.

Plaintiff church brought action against defendant breakaway church and its leader, alleging infringement of copyrights in works of plaintiff's founder.

Following appeal regarding plaintiff's trademark claims, 59 F.3d 902, the United States District Court for the Eastern District of California, Edward J. Garcia,

J., granted summary judgment in favor of defendants on plaintiff's copyright claims, and plaintiff appealed.

The Court of Appeals, Schroeder, Circuit Judge, held that:

(1) works by founder were not "works for hire"; (2) founder's works were not created as part of a corporate body; (3) fact issues existed as to whether founder assigned his common law copyrights to plaintiff; (4) plaintiff did not own copyrights in photographs that were published in plaintiff's magazine but were taken by unknown photographers or by photographer with no known connection to church; but (5) fact issues existed as to whether photographs taken by plaintiff's employees were works for hire. Affirmed in part, reversed in part, and remanded.

Before: SCHROEDER, NOONAN, and TASHIMA, Circuit Judges. SCHROEDER, Circuit Judge:

This litigation war between two rival churches concerns copyrights to the writings, photographs, and sound recordings of Swami Paramahansa Yogananda. The plaintiff, Self-Realization Fellowship Church

("SRF"), claims that it holds valid copyrights to all of the works. The defendants and admitted copiers are a breakaway church and its leader, Ananda Church of Self-Realization and James Walters ("Ananda"). They contend that none of the copyrights are valid.

The district court granted summary judgment in favor of Ananda. On appeal, SRF raises various issues. The most important are whether the works of a religious leader, living under a vow of poverty in the church he founded, can be considered "works for hire" or the works of a "corporate body" within the meaning of the 1909 Copyright Act and, in the alternative, whether SRF has adduced evidence from which a jury could conclude that a valid assignment of common law copyrights occurred.

With regard to Yogananda's writings and spoken lectures, we hold that the works are not works for hire or the works of a corporate body, so that the common law copyrights did not vest in the church as a matter of law. We hold that there are triable issues with regard to the purported assignments and remand for further proceedings on those issues. We also hold that there is a triable issue regarding whether some of the photographs involved in this appeal were works for hire.

BACKGROUND

Yogananda, a monk of the Swami order, founded SRF in 1935 when he arrived in *1325 California from India. Until his death in 1952, Yogananda lived in quarters that SRF provided and received from SRF a small monthly stipend. Yogananda served as SRF's president and as a member of its board of directors. While living at SRF, Yogananda wrote books and articles and gave religious lectures.

The lectures were recorded and later published by SRF. SRF arranged for the publication of Yogananda's books, and published the articles in its own magazine. SRF also published in its magazine various photographs of Yogananda and other SRF leaders.

In the district court, both parties introduced evidence of Yogananda's relationship with SRF and his intent regarding the ownership of his works and the copyrights to those works. For example, Yogananda observed a vow of poverty, which led him to assign all of his possessions to SRF in a written assignment dated May 28, 1935.

The assignment transferred to SRF Yogananda's "books, lessons, monthly araeceptum, furnitures, personal properties including shawls, blankets, portable temple of silence, my handwritings, typewriters, mimeograph machine, cooking utensils and all machinery, icebox, files, victrola, radio, and/or any other personal property which I may own and which is not described or enumerated herein." In 1939, Yogananda signed a standard SRF form agreeing to renounce any claim for compensation in exchange for "the privilege of being accepted as a worker" by SRF. SRF obtained copyrights on most, but not all, of Yogananda's published books in its own name, describing several of them as "works for hire." Of particular relevance to Ananda's position is the fact that in 1951

Yogananda entered into an agreement with an individual hired to translate six of his works into Spanish for distribution in Mexico.

The agreement provided that the "Mexican copyrights" to the English and Spanish versions of those six works would be obtained in Yogananda's name rather than the name of the translator.

Ten years after Yogananda's death, James Walters, also known as Sri Kriyananda, left SRF and formed Ananda, a rival church dedicated to the teachings of Yogananda. Ananda admits to copying the books, articles, recordings, and photographs involved in this appeal. SRF filed an infringement action in 1990.

We decided an earlier appeal regarding trademark claims in 1995. See Self- Realization Fellowship Church v. Ananda Church of Self-Realization, 59 F.3d 902 (9th Cir.1995).

The district court entered a final judgment disposing of all copyright claims in 1997, and this appeal followed.

DISCUSSION

Because all of the copied works were created before 1978, the Copyright Act of 1909 governs the validity of the initial copyrights. See Roth v.

Pritikin, 710 F.2d 934, 938 (2d Cir.1983). These initial statutory copyrights ran for a 28-year term. See

17 U.S.C. s 24 (repealed). Under the 1909 Act, the holder of the common law copyright at the time of publication, either the author or the author's assignee, was the party entitled to receive statutory protection. See Urantia Found.

v. Maaherra, 114 F.3d 955, 960 (9th Cir.1997). Assignments did not have to be in writing to be enforceable. See Magnuson v. Video Yesteryear, 85 F.3d 1424, 1428 (9th Cir.1996).

Authors could assign their common law copyrights "without the necessity of observing any formalities." Urantia Found.,114 F.3d at 960.

Blanket copyrights on magazines were sufficient to "protect all the copyrightable components of the work copyrighted" and gave to the copyright proprietor "all the rights which he would have if each part were individually copyrighted under" the Act. 17 U.S.C. s 3 (repealed). The weight of the case law has concluded that this means that a blanket copyright gives a magazine publisher rights in an individual contribution only if the publisher owns the common law copyright as the author of the contribution, or as the author's assignee. See Mail & Express Co. v. Life

Pub. Co., 192 F. 899, 900 (2d Cir.1912); The *1326 Williams & Wilkins Co.v. United States,

172 U.S.P.Q. 670, 675 (Ct.Cl.1972); Kinelow Publ'g Co. v. Photography in Bus., Inc., 270 F.Supp. 851, 853 (S.D.N.Y.1967); Ilyin v. Avon Publications, Inc., 144 F.Supp. 368 (S.D.N.Y.1956); Kaplan v. Fox Film Corp., 19 F.Supp. 780 (S.D.N.Y.1937).

The 1909 Act did not extend any protection to sound recordings, however.

With respect to Yogananda's recorded lectures, SRF claims a common law copyright enforceable under California law. See Klekas v. EMI Films, Inc., 150 Cal.App.3d 1102, 1108-09, 198 Cal.Rptr. 296 (1984) (explaining that before passage of the 1976 Act, works not protected by the federal copyright statute were protected by state law). Cal. Civ.Code s 980 extends common law copyright protection to sound recordings, and Cal. Civ.Code s 982 permits authors to transfer their rights in such works.

The copying at issue in this appeal took place at various times after 1962. Some works were copied during the initial copyright term, and some during the renewal term. The principal issues with respect to the works authored by Yogananda are, first, whether the works were "works for hire" or works produced by a "corporate body" within the meaning of the 1909 Act, and if not, whether Yogananda validly assigned his common law copyrights to SRF.

The district court held that the works were neither works for hire nor produced by a corporate body, and we agree. The district court further held that there was no valid common law copyright assignment to SRF. We disagree, and hold that SRF has presented triable issues regarding assignment.

Assuming that SRF can establish the validity of its initial copyright in each work, we must also decide a separate set of issues with respect to copying that took place during the works' renewal terms.

This is because under the 1909 Act, renewal rights revert in most circumstances to the author's next of kin where, as here, the author was not living at the time the initial copyright expired. We hold that SRF was not entitled to renew its copyrights in books authored by Yogananda.

We hold, however, that SRF was entitled to renew any valid initial copyrights in Yogananda's articles.

I. Works For Hire

[1][2] SRF contends that it holds valid initial and renewal copyrights in Yogananda's writings through the "work for hire" doctrine. See 17 U.S.C. s 26 (repealed) (stating that the word 'author' shall include an employer in the case of works made for hire). This circuit has summarized the work for hire doctrine as follows: "[W]hen one person engages another, whether as employee or as an independent contractor, to produce a work of an artistic nature, ... in the absence of an express contractual reservation of the copyright in the artist, the presumption arises that the mutual intent of the parties is that the title to the copyright shall be in the person at whose instance and expense the work is done." Lin-Brook Builders Hardware v. Gertler, 352 F.2d 298, 300 (9th Cir.1965).

To survive summary judgment on a claim of work for hire, SRF must "present some credible evidence that [Yogananda's] work was done at the instance and expense" of SRF. Dolman v. Agee, 157 F.3d 708, 712 (9th Cir.1998).

The Second Circuit has described the "instance and expense" test under the 1909 Act as an inquiry into whether "the motivating factor in producing the work was the employer who induced the creation." Playboy Enter., Inc. v. Dumas, 53 F.3d 549, 554 (2d Cir.1995). SRF has not introduced evidence that would demonstrate that it was at SRF's "instance" that Yogananda decided to write, teach, and lecture. Works motivated by Yogananda's own desire for self-expression or religious instruction of the public are not "works for hire." Furthermore, Nimmer explains that throughout much of the life of the 1909 Act, courts applied the work for hire doctrine only to traditional, hierarchical relationships *1327 in which the employee created the work as part of "the regular course of business" of the employer.

Melville B. Nimmer and David Nimmer, Nimmer on Copyright s 5.03[B][1][a][i] (1999).

In the last decade that the Act was effective, courts expanded the concept to include less traditional relationships, as long as the hiring party had "the right to control or supervise the artist's work." Id. We have described the rationale for the doctrine as a presumption that "the parties expected the employer to own the copyright and that the artist set his price accordingly." May v. Morganelli-Heumann & Assocs., 618 F.2d 1363, 1368 (9th Cir.1980). SRF's relationship with Yogananda was not the type of traditional relationship in which such a presumption would necessarily hold. Moreover, there was no evidence of supervision or control of Yogananda's work by SRF. Yogananda's works were thus not "works for hire."

II. Corporate Body

The 1909 Act also refers in its renewal provision, 17 U.S.C. s 24 (repealed), to works copyrighted by a "corporate body." We conclude that Yogananda did not create his works as part of a corporate body. Like many other courts, we have not had occasion to interpret this part of section 24 of the 1909 Act, but the Second Circuit has noted that "what authoritative commentary exists concerning the 'corporate body' provision of s 24 indicates that it has no application to works ... which are authored and produced by one identifiable person either as an employee for hire or as an independent author." Epoch Producing Corp. v. Killiam Shows, Inc., 522 F.2d 737, 748 (2d Cir.1975) (citing Barbara Ringer, Renewal of Copyright, in Report of the Register of Copyrights on the Revision of the U.S. Copyright Law, Study No. 31, at 136-37 (1960)).

The little case law that there is regarding the "corporate body" exception thus indicates that it has no application to cases in which a single, identifiable individual rather than a faceless corporate mass has created the work in question.

See Donaldson Publ'g Co. v. Bregman, Vocco & Conn, Inc., 375 F.2d 639, 643 (2d Cir.1967) (stating that the meaning of the corporate body clause in section 24 "is not entirely plain" but that "its scope is quite limited"). SRF offers no more reasonable interpretation of the phrase. We therefore conclude that the district court correctly held that SRF did not hold copyrights to Yogananda's works through the corporate body doctrine.

III. Assignment

Even if Yogananda did not create his works directly for SRF as works for hire or as part of a corporate body, SRF's initial copyrights are still valid if before publication SRF received from Yogananda an informal assignment of his common law copyrights. See Urantia Found., 114 F.3d at 960. Such assignments did not have to be in writing to be enforceable. See Magnuson, 85 F.3d at 1428 (stating that under the 1909 Act, common law copyrights could be transferred orally or by implication from the conduct of the parties). SRF points to several factual matters established in the record: the 1935 Assignment from Yogananda to SRF of all his possessions; Yogananda's vow of poverty; Yogananda's general acquiescence in SRF's decision to copyright many of his works in its name; and SRF's physical possession of the manuscripts.

These, SRF contends, constitute conclusive evidence that Yogananda informally assigned to SRF his common law copyrights in his books and periodical articles. Furthermore, SRF obtained initial statutory copyrights in its own name in the books written by Yogananda at issue in this appeal, and these copyrights are entitled to a presumption of validity under the 1909 Act because of the registration in SRF's name. See 17 U.S.C. s 209 (repealed) (stating that a certificate of copyright registration "shall be admitted in any court as prima facie evidence of the facts stated therein").

Ananda, for its part, submitted evidence showing that Yogananda obtained copyrights*1328 on other works, not at issue in this appeal, in his own name.

Ananda also offered an interpretation of Yogananda's vow of poverty indicating the vow was less than a complete renunciation of property rights. Ananda characterizes Yogananda's vow as "simple," rather than "solemn," arguing that Yogananda intended to retain some personal property and only wished to disavow profits.

Ananda also points to the evidence that Yogananda sought to obtain Mexican copyrights in his own name, thus suggesting that Yogananda never intended to transfer any of his common law U.S. copyrights to SRF.

The district court characterized as "critical" the fact that some of SRF's copyright certificates describe SRF as the owner of a work for hire rather than an assignee. This circuit has held, however, that a party's own descriptions of the nature of its copyright at the time of copyright registration or renewal is not conclusive. See Urantia Found., 114 F.3d at 963. Cf. Lin-Brook, 352 F.2d at 300 (holding that work could be a "work for hire" as a matter of law despite employer's decision to receive it through assignment from employee). Such descriptions may be self-serving, and the copyright laws are not to be applied mechanically, facilitating premature injection into the public domain, but rather in a "fair and non- formalistic" manner. See Urantia Found., 114 F.3d at 963.

The district court ultimately agreed with Ananda, accepting its interpretation of the vow of poverty and placing weight on the fact that not all of the works Yogananda produced during his lifetime were copyrighted in SRF's name. The existence of a transfer or assignment of common law copyright, however, is a factual question of the author's intent. See id. at 960. The 1935 assignment is not dispositive as to

Yogananda's writings after 1935, but it is relevant to this factual issue. While a jury may conclude that on balance the evidence demonstrates that Yogananda had no intent to transfer to SRF his common law copyrights, at the summary judgment stage, a district court is entitled neither to assess the weight of the conflicting evidence nor to make credibility determinations. See Anderson v. Liberty Lobby, Inc., 477 U.S. 242, 250, 106 S.Ct. 2505, 91 L.Ed.2d 202 (1986). SRF has introduced sufficient evidence to create a triable issue as to whether it held valid initial copyrights to Yogananda's writings through an informal assignment of Yogananda's common law copyrights. We therefore reverse the district court's grant of summary judgment with regard to any works copied in their initial copyright terms, and remand for further proceedings.

IV. Right of Renewal

With regard to writings copied during their renewal terms, SRF must establish its initial copyright and, in addition, establish that it was entitled to renew any validly obtained initial copyrights. The 1909 Act vested renewal rights in the author, if still living at the time the initial copyright term expired, or the author's next of kin or executor if the author was deceased. See 17 U.S.C. s 24 (repealed). The 1909 Act contained only four exceptions to this exclusive right of reversion.

A copyright owner who was not the original author could renew copyrights in (1) posthumous works, (2) periodical, encyclopedic, and composite works, (3) works copyrighted by a corporate body (other than as an assignee or licensee of the original author), and (4) works made for hire.

See id.

The word "posthumous," as it is used in copyright law and embodied in the first exception, is a term of art that refers to works unpublished at the time of the author's death in which the author at all times maintained the common law copyright. See Bartok v. Boosey & Hawkes, Inc., 523 F.2d 941, 944 (2d Cir.1975). SRF does not claim that this exception applies. The third and fourth exceptions do not apply because, as we have already held, the work for hire and corporate body doctrines do not apply to Yogananda's writings as a matter of law.

The only possible *1329 exception available to SRF at this point is the exception for "periodical, encyclopedic, and composite works."

With regard to books copied during their renewal terms, the district court's grant of summary judgment for Ananda must be affirmed. The books are not periodical, composite or encyclopedic works, nor does SRF contend that they are.

The articles that appeared in SRF's magazine, however, were published in a periodical. SRF itself held the copyright to each issue of the magazine. The 1909 Act allowed renewal by a copyright holder, even if not the original author or the author's next of kin, of copyrights to "periodical, encyclopedic, and collective works." 17

U.S.C. s 24 (repealed). A blanket copyright on a periodical protects its constituent parts as long as the publisher received the common law copyrights to those parts prior to publication. See 17 U.S.C. s 3 (repealed); Mail & Express, 192 F. at 900.

Thus, if SRF succeeds at trial in proving that Yogananda informally transferred to SRF his common law copyrights in his individual articles, SRF's blanket copyrights on each issue of its magazine were sufficient to give SRF rights to the articles as well. SRF would then have been entitled to renew these copyrights under the exception contained in section 24 for periodical works.

Until 1940, section 24 also permitted individual authors to renew copyrights in periodical contributions "when such contribution has been separately registered." In 1940, Congress deleted the separate registration requirement, permitting individual authors to renew copyrights in periodical contributions even if the only initial copyright on the work existed by virtue of the publisher's blanket copyright. Ananda argues that our decision in Abend v. MCA, Inc., 863 F.2d 1465 (9th Cir.1988), aff'd sub nom Stewart v. Abend, 495 U.S. 207, 110 S.Ct. 1750, 109 L.Ed.2d 184 (1990), holds that as a result of the 1940 amendment, only the author of a periodical contribution retains a renewal right in the work. This is incorrect. In Abend, we recognized that the 1940 amendment granted a new renewal right in individual authors of magazine contributions. See id. at 1470-71.

The discussion in Abend makes clear, however, that this new right did not extinguish the pre-existing right in the magazine publisher.

Congress was simply concerned about situations in which the publisher went out of business before the initial copyright expired, leaving no one to renew the copyright and thus injecting the work prematurely into the public domain. See id. at 1471 (citing H.R.Rep. No. 1612, 76th Cong.3d Sess. 1 (1940)).

Under the unambiguous terms of section 24 of the 1909 Act, SRF was entitled to renew any initial copyrights in periodical articles that it validly obtained through an informal assignment of Yogananda's common law copyrights. We therefore reverse the district court's grant of summary judgment with regard to all periodical articles, and remand for determination of the factual issues regarding assignment.

V. Recordings of Yogananda's Lectures

The 1909 Act does not cover sound recordings. SRF's rights, if any, in recordings of Yogananda's religious lectures are therefore governed by the common law of copyright and secured by California law. Cal. Civ.Code s 980 protects common law copyrights in sound recordings, and Cal. Civ.Code s 982 permits copyrights to be transferred.

California courts define "works for hire" in a similar fashion as federal courts interpreting the provisions of the Copyright Act of 1909. See Zahler v. Columbia Pictures Corp., 180 Cal.App.2d 582, 589, 4 Cal.Rptr. 612, 617 (1960) ("Where an employee creates something as part of his duties under his employment, the thing created is the property of his employer unless, of course, by appropriate agreement, the employee retains some right in or with respect to the product.").

The district court correctly rejected SRF's argument that Yogananda had created the recorded works as works for hire *1330 or as part of a corporate body, but incorrectly held that SRF had not presented a triable issue as to whether Yogananda ever assigned his common law copyrights in the recordings to SRF.

We reverse the district court on the ground that SRF has introduced evidence sufficient to create a triable issue regarding assignment. For reasons we have already explained, the evidence is conflicting on the critical issue of intent to transfer intellectual property rights.

VI. Photographs

The final category of works in which SRF claims valid copyrights are not works by Yogananda but rather photographs of Yogananda and another religious leader, taken by various third parties and published in SRF's magazine under its blanket copyright. For four of the photographs, SRF can identify no known photographer as the author. A fifth was taken by a man identified only by his name, Arthur Say, while the remaining photographs were taken by SRF employees Clifford Frederick and Durga Mata. The district court rejected SRF's claims that the photographs were taken as works for hire or by a corporate body, and held that SRF had not introduced a triable issue regarding assignment.

To succeed in a claim that the photographs were "works for hire," SRF must introduce evidence that the photographs were taken by an SRF employee or independent contractor at SRF's "instance or expense." Lin- Brook, 352 F.2d at 300. Likewise, in order to reach a jury on the issue of assignment, SRF must introduce evidence regarding the author's intent. Urantia Found., 114 F.3d at

960. For the four photographs with unknown authors, SRF cannot satisfy either of these requirements; the district court's grant of summary judgment must be affirmed. Similarly, SRF offered no evidence that Arthur Say was an SRF employee or independent contractor or that he intended to transfer his common law copyrights to SRF. We therefore also affirm the district court's grant of summary judgment with regard to the Arthur Say photograph.

The district court's grant of summary judgment with regard to the remaining photographs, all taken by SRF employees Clifford

Frederick and Durga Mata, was principally based on the court's rejection of the declaration of Ananda Mata, SRF's Secretary and Treasurer. The district court characterized Ananda Mata's declaration testimony as "insufficient" and "uncertain," and commented on the possible inaccuracy of Ananda Mata's memory.

We conclude that the district court discounted the declarations by making a determination of credibility. This is something the court should not undertake at the summary judgment stage. Liberty Lobby, 477 U.S. at 250, 106 S.Ct. 2505.

Ananda Mata's declarations set forth facts based on personal knowledge that give rise to a triable issue regarding whether the Frederick and Durga Mata photographs were created for SRF as works for hire. Ananda Mata stated in her first declaration that Frederick and Durga Mata were SRF employees and that photographing Yogananda constituted part of their employment.

Personal knowledge can be inferred from an affiant's position. See Sheet Metal Workers' Int'l Ass'n Local Union No. 359 v. Madison Ind., Inc., 84 F.3d 1186, 1193 (9th Cir.1996) (general manager's personal knowledge of hiring events could be presumed);

Barthelemy v. Air Lines Pilots Ass'n, 897 F.2d 999, 1018 (9th Cir.1990) (CEO's personal knowledge of various corporate activities could be presumed). As a corporate officer of SRF, Ananda Mata could be expected to know the identity of SRF employees and their tasks. Ananda Mata further stated in her declarations that the photographs were taken at her own instruction using equipment belonging to SRF. This constitutes personal knowledge of facts demonstrating that the photographs were taken at SRF's instance and expense.

*1331 We therefore hold that SRF has presented a triable issue as to whether the photographs taken by Frederick and Durga Mata were taken for SRF as works for hire. We reverse the district court's grant of summary judgment as to these works, and remand for further proceedings.

CONCLUSION

We affirm the district court's grant of summary judgment for Ananda with regard to books copied during their renewal terms, the photographs by unknown authors, and the photograph by Arthur Say.

We reverse and remand for further proceedings the claims of copyright infringement pertaining to the books copied during their initial terms, all periodical articles, the sound recordings, and the photographs by Clifford Frederick and Durga Mata.

AFFIRMED IN PART, REVERSED IN PART, AND REMANDED.

Each party to bear its own costs.

Licensing Check List

(This list is an intended reference and may not be exhaustive for every organization's needs).

1. Web-casting
2. Elements for congregational participation:
   a. Lyric downloads to be displayed in a bulletin or on a projector
   b. Copyrighted music/lead sheets
3. Use of copyrighted materials for conferences or seminars
4. Choir performances in church (if broadcast or recorded)
5. Concert performances (if broadcast or recorded)
6. Movie clips shown to groups
7. Downloading/Archiving (audio and video)
8. Music used in group exercise or dance classes
9. Incidental music (hold music, lobby music, or other music played in the church facility)
10. Use of copyrighted materials at social events away from the church's premises

11. Worship service DVD sales
12. Worship service CD sales
13. Concert DVD sales
14. Other items not covered by blanket licenses and requiring permission from the publisher or author of the work:
    a. Use of accompaniment CDs for public performances
    b. Use of handwritten musical arrangements
    c. Editing video or audio clips
    d. Synchronizing video with music
    e. Performance of dramatic musical works

Helpful Websites

For More Information)

United States Copyright Office http://copyright.gov

United States Patent & Trademark Office

http://www.uspto.gov

Church Copyright License http://www.ccli.com

Christian Copyright Solutions

http://www.copyrightsolver.com

Harry Fox http://harryfox.com

Music Publishers' Association http://mpa.org

American Society of Composers, Authors and Publishers http://www.ascap.com/index.aspx

Broadcast Music, Inc. http://bmi.com

Society of European Stage Authors and Composers

http://www.sesac.com

Cornell University's Public Domain Chart

http://copyright.cornell.edu/resources/publicdomain.cfm